CONTENTS

HINTERLANDS

Real
Aberystwyth

Also in the Real series

Real Cardiff – Peter Finch
Real Cardiff Two – Peter Finch
Real Newport – Ann Drysdale
Real Wrexham – Grahame Davies
Real Swansea – Nigel Jenkins

Forthcoming

Real Liverpool – Niall Griffiths
Real Merthyr – Mario Basini

Real
Aberystwyth

Niall Griffiths

Series Editor: Peter Finch

seren

Seren is the book imprint of
Poetry Wales Press Ltd
Nolton Street, Bridgend, Wales
www.seren-books.com

© Niall Griffiths 2008
Series Introduction © Peter Finch 2008

The right of Niall Griffiths to be identified
as the Author of this Work
has been asserted in accordance with the
Copyright, Designs and Patents Act, 1988.

ISBN 978-1-85411-447-1

A CIP record for this title is available from
the British Library

The publisher works with the financial assistance
of the Welsh Books Council

Printed by Bell & Bain, Glasgow

SERIES INTRODUCTION

Aberystwyth is now a real place. I'm in the town again to try to get a new feel for it, to check out some of the things that Niall Griffiths has discovered. I've been coming here professionally for decades – to the Library, the Books Council, the Books Centre, for meetings of the Academi at the Conrah in Chancery, for debates with writers and publishers in bars and cafés and rooms in hotels – but those have been purposeful arrivals and never rambling tours. When I first came here in the fifties, as a child of eleven, brought by my parents in a coach with scratchy seats and cream doors, I thought I'd landed on the moon. How could that be a beach, that colour? Those ice cream shops. And that truncated pier, a battered hang-on from a 1920s film. Did people holiday here in this so a Welsh place? They certainly did.

Aberystwyth is no burgeoning city, redevelopment is minimal, its skyline is not full of cranes. The sense of alienation you get in places like Cardiff and even Swansea is absent here. Aber wanted to be the capital of Wales when that honour was up for grabs in 1955 and put up a good case – geographically central, Welsh-speaking, full of institutions. But there was more money in Cardiff. Business wins. Same thing happened again almost fifty years later when the Assembly was created. That institution also followed the money. Aber now contents itself with the title of unofficial capital. Welsher than anywhere bar Caernarfon. More cultured than Pontcanna. A place you can hold. Alternative capital. Gay capital. Student capital on sea. New Brighton. The hippie Biarritz of Wales. In 1994 Aberystwyth elected former Incredible String Band member Rose Simpson as mayor. This town does not slumber quietly. Indigenous population is around 12,000 to which can be added more than 7,000 students in term time. Physically it is dominated by its institutions, rising in a tiered stack inland. Bronglais Hospital, the National Library, illuminated at night and looking like a Welsh version of the White House, and then the vast and brutalist Penglais Campus of the Arts Centre, Science Park and University.

Down at the harbour, halfway between the northern Constitution Hill and the southern Penparcau outcrop, on the top of which stands Pen Dinas, an iron age fort, I watch the fishing boats unload shellfish, lobsters and spider crabs. Basket after basket. They go into tanks and get driven to Spain. A half life left for a few more days. Better price there than here.

Aberystwyth is actually a very literary place. In his excellent guide *The Literary Pilgrim In Wales* Meic Stephens lists around thirty greats who have association. Everyone from Richard Hughes to the Marxist poet T.E. Nicholas. The house of Caradoc Evans is in Queens Square (plaque on the wall courtesy of the Rhys Davies Trust 'Er Cof Am Caradoc Evans 1878-1945' – WKD sticker in the window above it). Gwyn Jones, translator of the *Mabinogion*, had a house in Sea View Place. John Barnie, poet and former editor of *Planet* lives in Comins Coch. Niall Griffiths in nearby Penrhyncoch. I walk up along the edge of South Beach with its vaguely yellow sand and mixed detritus left by holiday makers, penniless students and druggies.

It's difficult to remember sometimes that this place, founded as a centre of power when Strongbow built his castle, a place of shipbuilding, bigger than Cardiff in the seventeenth century, a centre for lead and silver ripped from the Ceredigion hills, a market town full of sheep and cattle sales, was largely a Victorian invention – at least that part of the town that remains. When the railways arrived so did the tourists. Grand hotels were built. The pier and the funicular railway constructed. People still holiday here, working class from Birmingham and the West Midlands, staying in caravan parks in the hills beyond the town. Aberystwyth is their nearest piece of sea. They come in droves to wander the clifftop golf links, ride the Rheidol narrow-gauge steam railway to Devil's Bridge and gawp at the pre-tech Google earth that is the camera obscura on the top of Constitution Hill.

At Castle Point I pass the 1923 war memorial, an engraved, name-decked pillar which faces the sea. Death remembered in victory. Angel atop carrying triumphal wreath and olive branch, edifice fronted with a perfectly formed female nude displaying erect cast bronze nipples, humanity freeing herself from the chaos of war. Aber is a town of contrasts. On nearby Trefechan Bridge, site of the Welsh Language Society's first ever protest in 1963, five new millennium members were arrested in a 2002 protest centred around the unveiling of a memorial plaque. Why in Aberystwyth? Intellectual capital, centre of thought and encouragement, place where it first became possible to do everything in Welsh, to take the language out from the hearth and home and engage it with the modern world. Since 1963 there have been two language Acts and a reversal in Welsh's downward spiral. Statistics steady. Learners swell their numbers. But the woods have not yet been cleared.

On New Promenade I pass the Old College, built in 1872 as a hotel but turned instead into the first University in Wales. History, maths, physics. Twenty-six students. The principal was Thomas Charles Edwards and his statue now stands out front. He was a writer, and a Presbyterian preacher. God hovered ever near.

Aber Ystwyth, mouth of the Ystwyth, the river that pours through the town centre and fills the harbour. But then that's actually the River Rheidol. Perversely, the Ystwyth skirts the town to the south. Aberrheidol. Doesn't sound right.

You can't get lost in Aberystwyth. Steal something and they'll see you. Have an affair and you'll be spotted. And the louche trollops of the town, despite Malcolm Pryce, do not wear stove pipe hats. The druids don't run the milk bars. I couldn't find the ice cream shops. At the top of town by the roundabouts of Llanbadarn Fawr I stop to watch the traffic drift in. More arrive than leave, so it seems. I watch the drivers spin their steering wheels, mostly trying simultaneously to do something else: talking on phone, reading a message, eating an apple, lighting a cigarette, drinking coke, unscrewing a bottle cap, texting, retuning to Radio Cymru, poking the sat nav, opening a Mars Bar, reading a letter, consulting an atlas, shouting, fixing their make-up, singing 'Mae Hen Wlad Fy Nhadau', scratching their ears, hunting in the glove compartment, eating peanuts, adjusting their cravats, dictating bits of their next novel into a digital notebook, reciting poetry. Could be Niall. He does poetry. He also does excellent fiction. But the book you hold today goes beyond that. *Real Aberystwyth*. Essential reading if you live here and pretty good even if you don't.

Peter Finch

Going N. from the Tyvy about 25 miles, we came to Abrystwyth, that is to say, the town at the mouth of the River Ystwyth. This town is enriched by the coals and lead, which is found in its neighbourhood, and is a populous, but a very dirty, black, smoky place, and we fancied the people looked as if they lived continually in the coal or lead mines. However, they are rich, and the place is very populous.

Daniel Defoe, *A Tour Through the Whole Island of Great Britain,* Penguin, 1971 (first published 1726)

Aberystwyth is one big pub with lots of corridors.
Richard Burton, allegedly

PREFACE

I was ill; travel sickness, probably. I threw up in a plastic bag, all over the sandwiches. Everything required for the holiday in Tenby had been packed except for the motion sickness pills so a roadmap was consulted and it was discovered that, with a small detour, what appeared to be the largest town between where we were in Wales at that moment and our destination of Pembrokeshire could be reached with just a little additional time. So we drove into that town. Parked up, somewhere. One parent went in search of medicine and the ingredients to make more sandwiches and the other parent took me and my siblings down to look at the sea.

I was eight, I think. I remember very little of that day except a long curve of grand buildings and a big green hill with another building atop it and a sea that was blue, strikingly blue, a very different shade to the gravy Mersey or Dee that I was used to. We didn't stay there long, only enough time for me to swallow some pills and for us all to eat some hastily-assembled cheese butties. And then, two decades later, and looking for somewhere to continue my unenthusiastic studies (a postgrad degree, compared to the horrors of a proper job, is much the lesser of two evils) and, more importantly, reeling from the unhappy end of an affair and needing to flee from a place suddenly throbbing with loss and, additionally, harbouring a desire to both find and put down roots, I remembered that hill and the sweep of the bay and those buildings with the sunlight glinting off their glass and that blue, blue sea. Remembered, too, the sense of that town as being remote, isolate, difficult to reach; a place at the end of somewhere, a terminus. Not somewhere you'd ever just pass through (although that's exactly what I did, on that pukey, restless journey).

I've lived in Aberystwyth or it's environs now for nearly fourteen years. The town isn't in my blood – I wasn't born here, and the Cymric stuff in my veins has bled out from north Wales, not mid – but it's on my skin; I know its pubs and offices and squats and ginnels and some of its people and some of its history, its stains and decals and features, both guidebook and covert. There's a strange draw to the place; get off the train and you can't go any further. Stand on the promenade and the next landmass is Ireland and, after that, America. Mountains pile up behind you and you feel that you can't go back into their bulwark mass but the sea, there, in front of you, is a blue world of possibility. And between that and the giant rocks is this small, intriguing town, its lanes and alleys and doorways a jumbled alphabet waiting to be re-assembled.

Which isn't to say that it's Trumpton, of course; one of the ways in which it can be read as a mini-city is the presence in it of those frustrations and longings usually associated with a larger conurbation and their expression in various forms of abuse. Also, whilst the general feel of the place is a lot more expansive and open than can be found in most other towns of its size, a kind of 'small-town mentality' can inevitably be seen here, on occasion very conspicuously; jealousy and resentment are fostered, nurtured even, allowed to seethe. The urge to escape takes on ugly shapes. Concomitant with this is the fallacious boast: 'I'm stuck here, so I'll convince myself that it's the best place in the world, and I'll tell everybody else that until they agree with me'.

Aberystwyth is neither a paradise or a prison. It's a unique place in a striking setting with, as *The Rough Guide to Wales* says, an 'anarchic soul'. It's the place where the Welsh Language Movement (Cymdeithas yr Iaith Gymraeg) grew its more modern, militant stripes; it's the only place where the Queen has been forced to terminate a royal visit (loyal subjects? In Aberystwyth? Pah). It is what you make of it; it supplies the materials, and what you build with them is entirely up to you. There are as many 'real' Aberystwyths as there are inhabitants of this peculiar, fascinating town.

I no longer get car-sick, and the affair I'm fully immersed in now and have been for some years and which began in Aberystwyth gets stronger and better as it develops. Mist is beginning to roll off the mountain behind the house and some sparrows are squabbling in the lane; I can see the yellow eyes of a cat in the hedge, watching them, and the cruciform shape of a kite circling a leafless tree. This could end badly. But then again it could not; the sparrows can fly away.

Big thanks are due to Peter Finch for commissioning this book, and for his advice and encouragement (and for getting the 'Real' ball rolling in the first place). Mick Felton and all at Seren, too. Were I to make an exhaustive list of all the people I need and would like to thank, the book you're holding would be twice as long; suffice then to say that, if you're not mentioned in the text and if at any time over the past fourteen years or so I've ever laughed with you or drank with you or listened intently to whatever you've told me, then you have my undying gratitude. God bless yiz all.

As the dragon made from red wire that once stood opposite Y Cŵps pub on the main artery into the town proper used to say: Croeso.

INTRODUCTION: NOT A CITY

The entry for Aberystwyth on the craptowns website[1] is brilliant. Written by 'Abugh Girl', in alluring and unpunctuated Wenglish, it reads:

> Aberystwyth called Ab-ugh by locals boys in the hood (hoods from b-wise like) forget all the drygs available at dryg-booths on street corners as in 'grits'[2] + monged out drug filled girls singing welsh folk songs in pybs – abugh is home to the ugliest flats/new homes/car parks/card shops in history, all looking like they've been built by drunken donkeys with lollypop sticks.

I love this. It has the clipped delivery of the truly pissed off. I know nothing about 'Abugh Girl' beyond this entry, but, whoever she is, she's got a talent. She goes on, splendidly:

> Shops terrible, now full of baggies that would have done the Stone Roses proud circa 1990. Locals ffed yp with students and brummie holiday makers who take it in turns to piss on the doors of WH Smith, clog yp the pavements, puke over the cash points. Top class castle, sea front all ruined with flags, crazy paving, concrete tubs full o tulips (never fully grown). To top it all off – crazy golf's closed.

Sadly, that's all there is. I could read entire novels of Abugh Girl's foot-stamping rants. It's good stuff. And, in her mention of students and Brum holiday-makers taking over and contributing to the town's uglification, she brushes against a peculiarly Aber paradox; the anonymity on offer in its smallness. Or, rather, less anonymity and more the wash of identity in a town with such a protean population, dominated as it is by students and transient tourists. In that, Aberystwyth can have the feel of a city, which it isn't, although driving down into it from the top of Penglais Hill on a clear day, it can look a little bit like one. As it can do if you climb Constitution Hill and look straight ahead to Pen Dinas and then let your eye drift slowly left to take in the ranked terraces beyond the town proper criss-crossing the far hills in the haze some miles away. Shrunken city or swollen town, that's what it can feel like. That's what it is.

The census takers[3] divide the town into seven wards: Aberystwyth Bronglais, population 1,928; Canol (central), 2,177; Gogledd (north), 1,957; Penparcau, 3,098; Rheidol, 2,457; South, 3,347; and West, 3,381. That's 18,335 in total. When the student population of roughly 9,000 is added on, it's still hardly a metropolis, and indeed I have stayed in smaller cities in Wales (St. David's, St. Asaph), in England (Wells), and even, further afield, in smaller capitals (Nuuk). And of course the whole city concept is as much an imaginary one as it is politically designated, which is to say that, wherever human beings gather, all the machinery of the civic is corralled into dealing with the fall-out of their interactions. The issue, really, is only one of degrees (which, in some respects, is true not just of cities but of nations themselves, or so our leaders would have us think); degrees of ethnicity; of how much earth must be appropriated for landfill sites. Degrees of identity, too, which for a Welsh town are crucial, especially one so racially mixed and of so small a fixed populace. The *Rough Guide to Wales* depicts the town as 'the capital of the sparsely populated middle of the country', and that it is, but demographical relativism doesn't really explain why, in one night, I can drink with an Irishman and an American, dance with an Englishwoman, drink more with a Finn and a Pole, shake hands with a Sikh, get served beer by a Scot, buy a kebab from a Turk and get taxi'd home by a Greek. Nor does it explain why a snapshot of St. James's Square or Terrace Road at 3 a.m. on any given Saturday morning could've been taken in any town or city across these woeful, wonderful islands; see the bared and blotchy legs; the blow-up dolls carried like banners of buffoonery; the burly men in dresses (hilarious, because no rugby player has ever gone out drinking dressed as a woman, ever); the tumbleweeds of chip paper; the fraught and yellow-jacketed constabulary; the pastel-shirted lads like a tube of Opal Fruits (oops, sorry, Starbursts); the pools of spew and blood (better to see them now than in the hungover morning, putting you off your paper, tea, and fried egg roll).

Look at the light with which that scene is lit; the bleached spill from the take-aways and the lilac lightning of the meat wagons and the ochre sodium of the streetlights and the pulsing rainbows from the clubs and bars. It's oneiric; it's fantastic. It suggests that this book would be better off titled in the negative – Unreal Aberystwyth. For the town seems to lend itself to endless re-invention, to fabulous interpretation; to the Anglo-Welsh Chandlerisms of Malcolm Pryce's books; to the supposed resting place of the Holy Grail; to a haunt of panthers; to a site of miraculously-healing waters; to the gay capital of Wales (as coined by Mike Parker, who told me that he 'kind of hoped that if I put it in print often enough, it might come true'). The American website haxan.com (which describes 'Aberystwyth, Wales' as a town 'on the west coast of England') carries a story from the early 1900s about frequent sightings of red-eyed, green-furred ghost-dogs haunting the town. Doyle's *The Hound of the Baskervilles* had been published shortly before but *The Objective Reporter*, a local paper of the time, dismissed any claims of detective-fiction-influenced hallucinatory paranoia with these words:

> Although the dog may have been a vision inspired by Doyle's story, it's been noted for years that the area around the town has been the haunting ground of many a spirit and home to the fairy folk in time gone by. Perhaps [the sightings have been] shaped by the written word but the power behind them may have been fashioned by the supernatural.

Such visions continued until 1934 when Hubert Maxwell, a respected banker, was attacked by a ghost dog in his own home; in his words, the beast was 'larger than most with hell's flint in it's eyes and the glow of the damned in its fur'.

Well, maybe. Perhaps the disused mines that turn the hills surrounding the town into Swiss cheese do harbour demon dogs and phantom felids. But, curiously, animals of a very real sort do seem drawn to the town; the sepia postcard of an elephant bathing in the sea (elephants were, apparently, once housed in enclosures behind what is now the Belle Vue Hotel) is well known and has sold millions, but in 2006 a truck carrying a rhinoceros and a hippopotamus was involved in a crash and had to be temporarily abandoned in the Dole layby, four miles or so outside the town[4]. What is it with Aberystwyth and pachyderms? And the sea teems; dolphins, whales, sunfish, leatherback turtles, basking sharks, they've all been spotted here. (I saw a seahorse once, too.)

And some of those elephants are pink. And are ridden by green monkeys. And some of the birds talk; the pigeons beg for spare change, and the crows make whispered threats. And there are insects, millions of them thrashing through walls and skin as the DT's take hold because the culture, here, or certain aspects of it anyway, is rich in drink and drugs[5], from the vodka promotion nights to the '2/4/1' happy-hours in the studenty bars to the damp hills around million-nippled by mushrooms. Which is just as it's always been, really; barelegged woad-heads, buzzing on mead and psilocybin, would keep bleary watch atop Pen Dinas for the approach of their trading partners from another, similar land beyond the waves (although it's not difficult to picture their chemical transport as conducted with much greater dignity and grace than its twenty-first century counterpart). Indeed, as well as drugs, *dros y mor* has been a defining feature of human movement and aspiration here, on the western windy edge of Eurasia, and although silt and national maritime decline now prevent the *Good Brig Credo* or the *Albion* from ferrying passengers over to Quebec or New York (passage three pounds with five shilling head money), there evolved many other methods of taking people over, or inviting them across, the always-angry waves. The university's presence does not explain this flux. I don't know what does. But it only becomes pointless to look when you start to expect an answer.

So an 'anarchic soul', then, this place has, and I'd agree with that; it's why I still live here, and why I don't see a vast difference neither immediate nor deeper between the town where I now live and the much bigger civic centre a hundred miles or so to the north where I was born and, with its million diverse fingers, moulded by. Stand on the promenade, look west, and you'll feel the mountains pressing at your back and you'll understand that, unless whatever you're fleeing from is strong and vicious and vengeful enough to send you skimming like a slate shard over the sea, you must remain here in your skin, slowly accepting the growing soul within. It's the end of the land, and the sea before you is never calm. As the old maps so enticingly have it: Here Be Dragons. The Queen herself knows that; the intensity of the protests that greeted her visit to open the newly-extended National Library forced her to turn back. I'll drink to that (as many did).

Hers is just one story from the human seethe in this not-quite-a-city place. There are many, many more.

notes

1. www.idler.co.uk/crap
2. Can't think what she's referring to here.
3. See www.statistics.gov.uk
4. See Dylan Davies (A).
5. Yes, I know that drug-fuelled hallucinations aren't as literal as I've suggested they are. It's poetic licence.

APPROACHING

FROM THE NORTH: A487

We'll begin, on this road, at Tal-y-bont, because beyond that the civic hub becomes Machynlleth (and that's for someone else to write about), and anyway Tal-y-bont's interesting. It's home to the offices of the publisher and printer, Y Lolfa. The hills surrounding it once played host to wonderful, ecstatic parties. It has two pubs. Somewhere around it Mihangel Morgan wrote *Melog*; in Chris Meredith's translation, a beguiling, beautiful, baffling novel (even better in the original Welsh, I'm sure). And it is, apparently, surrounded by panthers.

It's late July when I walk there, on the track (hardly a road) that runs through Elerch/Bontgoch. It's been sunny of late, but not today, and low-slung clouds have brought a horrible humidity. Those clouds mutter about rain too so I wear jeans and a t-shirt and a baseball hat and am, quite quickly, dripping with sweat. Thirsty flies try to land and drink on my face. There are kites, swallows, swifts, the ubiquitous crows. Once, at the edge of a field on this lane, I watched crows scavenge a freshly-dead sheep; they formed a stabbing black bundle on its face like the flies are trying to do on mine. The back of the sheep was a burst of unravelled guts, fanned out like the tentacles of a squid. It was brutal and savage, the *veldt* in miniature. God knows how the sheep died, but it's been happening a lot, around here. There might be big cats about. In November 2006 there were seven reported sightings in a two-week period in the Tal-y-bont area[1]. Ripped sheep have been found wedged in high branches of trees. I once spoke to a vet who'd studied feline predators in Africa and he told me that the wounds he'd seen on the carcasses of some

of these sheep were remarkably similar to those inflicted by a leopard; lions attempt a single lethal bite (to the spine or windpipe, say), but leopards prefer sheer mechanical damage, and their gape is huge. The *Cambrian News* carried tips on what to do if you encounter one: 'Act human; talk and make noise as you walk. Do not walk away quietly. Allow the cat to move away at its own pace and in its own direction. Do not attempt to follow the cat'[2].

So I'm in panther land. I'm being stalked, maybe. Except the hairs can't rise on the back of my neck because they're sweatlogged to the skin. The silence here is broken only by the whistle of a breeze across the field. I can see windmills on the hills – they're new, these ones. They're cropping up everywhere (more on this later), their fins front-crawling above the peaks and ridges. There is a feeling here – as there is to most of the valleys and hills outlying Aberystwyth – of tremendous, dizzying antiquity; of age only measurable in terms that we cannot properly grasp, that make our minds either spin or retreat to contemplate. I look around for the derelict and deserted house that appears in John Barnie's poem 'At Craig-y-Pistyll'[3], which imagines the final inhabitant who 'heard the silence as defined by leaves' and who stayed on there to witness 'people giving up and leaving the door open without looking back/Following the bitter jutting of their jaws'. I don't think it's here, though; I'd imagine it's more behind me and to the right, towards Salem, towards the place I've come from.

It's very humid. My light blue t-shirt is now navy with perspiration. I pause to look up at the darting swifts and see a buzzard chasing them. He's got no chance. Devil Birds, swifts were once called; the sudden way they shriekingly appear when the sun starts to sink, their speed, the way they seem to exult in flight and caused fright. Their incredible energy; easy to see why they were thought demonic. They're amongst my favourite birds, as is the buzzard, up there, who after a few clawed flicks at blurs rolls away with what looks to be a pissed-off shrug of the shoulders.

There's a pinprick of pain on the back of my hand. I look and see a fat cleg fly suck and then fly away. A spot of blood appears. Cleg flies I do not like.

Traffic can be heard now, on the A487, and I enter Tal-y-bont. It's a pretty, quirky village, with the two Lions on the green and Ruth Jan Evans's striking mural on the gable end of the terrace, at the moment sadly partly obscured by scaffolding. Y Lolfa's offices are in what looks like it used to be an old school or police station, on the road out towards Eglwys Fach. I go in and climb up towards Robat Gruffydd's eyrie of an office.

Y Lolfa[4] is now the biggest employer in Tal-y-bont. Robat, Swansea-born, moved here in 1966 when he got married, and he remembers sixteen shops and a woollen mill (to be fair, Tal-y-bont is still blessed with amenities, compared to other nearby villages of similar size), 'two banks, two butchers, a smithy, a cobbler, three or four general shops, [and] the bars in the public houses were full of farm labourers who kept village folklore alive'[5]. He writes that he 'feels sad, rather than proud, to say that Y Lolfa is the biggest employer in the village today', and I can see his point, but there is, still, a sense of Welsh cultural community to Tal-y-bont, exemplified by Ruth's mural and, of course, Y Lolfa itself. Robat tells me that, at university, he became involved in Cymraeg politics and wanted to start a press that could express that, which was 'as much a result of the period as any clear ambition I might have had', but he's being endearingly modest here; I will later be told by a source I won't name that Robat has achieved something of a legendary status in Welsh political activism; that he and Gwilym Tudur, of Aberystwyth's Siop y Pethe, when students at Bangor, were so angered at the second-class treatment of Welsh speakers that at their graduation ceremony they walked off stage without accepting their degrees. Gwilym went on to open a bookshop, Robat to run Y Lolfa. Perhaps not a spectacular protest, especially in the militant context of the time, but laudably self-sacrificial nonetheless.

Robat moved to the Aberystwyth area not due to any sort of search for 'Abercuawg'[6] but because his wife, Enid, lived there. Her parents offered financial support to set up his printing press but also, at that time, Labour government grants under the Rural Regeneration Scheme (similar to today's Objective One funding) allowed him to purchase machinery at a 50 per cent discount. He moved into the Emporium, the building now muralised, which was once a warehouse to store goods for the local shops; a decade later he moved the press up the road to the old police station (I was right).

He tells me that Y Lolfa began 'as a printing service, really', and that their first publication was a volume of poems by Eirwyn Pontshan (he's on the mural, drinking milk; his consumption of alcohol was, apparently, industrial). The most successful early book was an aid to learning Welsh called, predictably, *Welsh is Fun!* (popularisation spreads the appeal, of course). Robat was on Trefechan Bridge in 1962 (more on that later). He reckons that Cymdeithas yr Iaith is 'now part of the establishment, and tamer than it was then' – which he's entitled to say – but he does stress how much has been achieved; bilingual road signs, for example, didn't exist back then. Everything was in English.

Y Lolfa also printed promotional posters for bands, etc. Cook books sold well (including Helen Smith Twiddy's *Celtic Cookbook*, which is great[7]), as did the stuff aimed at the tourist trade. Wasn't there an irreconcilability there, between that and the more militant Welsh stuff being published, like John Jenkins's *Prison Letters*? Robat says no; that they were always presenting Wales through Welsh eyes and that they were in a run-down Welsh area, employing Welsh people, so why shouldn't they take the tourist pound to support the area? Fair enough. *Chwarae teg*. He says that he's now moving more towards the English language, but that he doesn't want to step on the toes of other Welsh publishers, like Seren or Parthian. Humorous books and books of a local nature are selling well, but the biggest sellers are those of Welsh interest written in English – Ned Thomas's books, for example (we'll meet Ned later). Still, there's very little media interest in this kind of stuff, he says; not even Richard Booth's autobiography, although it sold well, received more than a paucity of reviews.[8]

The 2005 catalogue is impressive; *yn Gymraeg* – Caryl Lewis, Rocet Arwel Jones, Robat himself, Mihangel Morgan, Lyn Ebenezer; *yn Saesneg*, Mike Parker's *Neighbours from Hell*, Meic Stevens's *Solva Blues*, Paul Ferris's biography of Dylan Thomas. What of the future? More of the same; honing, selecting, etc. The experienced editor Gwen Davies has recently decamped here. They're dependent on a Welsh-language readership and audience and there is a perpetual fight for the language (there's a resigned kind of angry sadness to Robat as he says this, which will be true of most workers in Welsh I speak to whilst researching this book). If the language flourishes, so will Y Lolfa. There is a brain drain from rural Wales to Cardiff. 'Legitimised language usage is all very well,' Robat says, 'but if there isn't a social base…'.

He trails off. Then gets re-animated when he tells me about *Y Byd*, the proposed daily Welsh-language newspaper that has the support of Huw Edwards, Gruff Rhys, Jan Morris and other Cymric luminaries. It will have offices in the north, the south, and the middle of the country. Robat's on the board, although it'll have little to do with Y Lolfa. The left-wing politics of the enterprise are impeccable; to oppose the monopoly of the Murdoch/Mirror group (which produces the two Welsh dailies, the *Post* and the *Western Mail*), and, obviously, spread the appeal of a minority language (the promotional material tabulates the extent of European minority-language newspapers, from Frisian in the Netherlands to Romansch in Switzerland). Kyffin Williams, the late artist, with his customary generosity, donated a painting to auction for funds. And if they're offered help by institutions with let's say less-than-squeaky-clean reputations? 'Well, there are core aims that can't be overturned without the agreement of all co-directors. It'll very much be a democratic, egalitarian enterprise'. I find myself saying and thinking *chwarae teg* a lot when I'm with Robat.

Despite the open windows, it's still hot in Robat's high office. We need several cold drinks. On our way to the pub we call in at Ruth Jen Evans's studio/workshop, an old shoe shop in the centre of the village. It's a great place, crammed with lino-cuts and woodcuts and paints and easels and brushes. Her recent work is inspired by the poetry of T.H. Parry-Williams; 'the emphasis is on colour and quality and the figure, form is less apparent', Ruth writes in *On Paper* (see 'Works Consulted); 'the printing process is important in this work. The experimenting and decisions are made at the press rather than on the printing "plate" or in the sketch book'. It's great, ghostly stuff. Robat loves Ruth's work; so do I. She was born nearby in Penbontrhydybeddau, did the Cardiff thing, but quickly returned to her roots. Check out her website canysrufus@siopsgidie.fsnet.co.uk. And go to Tal-y-bont and gaze at her mural. It's fantastic.

At the pub, Robat fills me in on his personal history. His mother was German-Jewish and fled to Wales during the pre-WWII pogroms. Her mother died at Ravensbruck. Both his parents were Egyptologists. Kate Bosse-Griffiths was his mother's name, and she always loved the Welsh people for being so unlike the upper-class Germans she knew; she loved their open-ness and intelligence and friendliness. She learned Welsh, and wrote two novels in that language published by Gomer. Robat's credentials, like the beers, get better and better and better.

Between Tal-y-bont and Aberystwyth lies Bow Street: Spar, school, garage, butchers, post office, chippy, two pubs. According to a man I once met who traced people's family trees for a living, it's called Bow Street because, at the time of naming, it was a village full of prostitutes who worked the busy harbour-side over the hill in Aberystwyth. The main red-light district in London at that time was Bow Street, so the name was simply copied. Which might be a fanciful story, but it's odd, that old English name in the midst of so many old Welsh ones. And does it really matter if it's accurate or not? It's a good story. I believe it.

Leave Bow Street. Go under the railway bridge. Pass the Comins Coch turning where, recently, I witnessed a sheepdog get hit by a 4x4. The noise was horrific. The whole thing was horrific. The dog pretty much burst. Climb the hill past Waunfawr and you'll see the town all spread out below you and then pass the uni on your left and the entrance to the National Library and Bronglais hospital and there's Y Cŵps pub and you're in town.

FROM THE EAST: A44

We'll start here at Goginan, because beyond that your civic centres are Llanidloes and Rhayader. Actually no, we won't start at Goginan, because that'll be written about in the 'Hinterlands' section, as will our mountain, Pumlumon, but we'll begin at the eastern foothills of that massif where the 'ELVIS' rock has become a prominent Ceredigion landmark. It's like 'welcome home' bunting; once past it, I know that my house is within reach. I know I'm safe. I'm not the only one to feel this way; Patricia Duncker's essay in the Parthian collection *A Bit on the Side* talks about climbing Pumlumon in a car where

> the sign says MOUNTAIN LAMBS ARE SWEETER. More adorable, or more delicious? Or both? Then, unaccountably, the rocks before me proclaim ELVIS LIVES... I climb past the Red Kite visitor's centre and I know that beyond the dark folds of these curving hills there is nothing left except the sea... Aberystwyth curls around the bay, folded in silence and sleep.

In truth, the rock proclaims just 'ELVIS' – it is not followed by its serendipitous anagram. If I asked around, I'm sure I could discover its provenance; who wrote it, when, and why. But I don't want to know. I prefer the mystery.[9]

There's a hailstorm of Old Testament ferocity when I go to photograph the rock. It's actually in Powys, but is recognised as the gatepost to Ceredigion. In a puddle at the side of the road we spot some frogspawn; our garden pond is failing to attract frogs so we put some spawn into a bottle to take home (it will hatch, and we'll have five tadpoles, and they'll become tiny frogs, and then a larger frog will appear and cannibalise them all). This isn't panther country, it's people country; megaliths are scattered on the hills, other signs of ancient settlements, and hikers frequently get lost. The thin soil boils with the bones of the vanquished of Glyndŵr. Jim Perrin patrols these uplands; Ken Jones, with a headful of haiku, notes how the mountain is 'soaked in every kind of wetness, for days and even weeks on end'[10]. More on these fine men and writers later, but it's strange, isn't it, how bleakness, how inhospitableness, even hostility, attracts us? In terms of evolutionary determinism, we should be repulsed by Pumlumon; it has no shelter, no dryness, nothing beyond rye grass will grow there. Its lakes and rivers may have fish but its game is elusive and scarce. Rain batters its peaks so fiercely that the water bounces back thigh-high. We should avoid it like we avoid quagmire, and yet we don't. In fact, it's easy to become smitten with it, drawn to the roar of its contours. We're a strange specie.

Leave the mountain (we'll return to it later), and enter a different weather[11]. Ahead of you lies Ponterwyd, and the George Borrow Inn, named, apparently, to spite the man who would only tarry a night there on his way to Devil's Bridge and who wrote sarcastically of 'that

remarkable personage in whom were united landlord, farmer, poet, and mighty fine gentleman – the master of the house'[12]. It's still a pub, intermittently popular, but welcome at all times in one of the storms that frequently strafe the hills and ridges round about. After Ponterwyd, Goginan. After that, Penllwyn Capel Bangor, with its two pubs, both great, one haunted and microbreweried. Then the accident blackspot of the Gelli Angharad/Lovesgrove roundabout where the fields on the left host an annual agricultural show and, once, the National Eisteddfod. Then Glan yr Afon industrial estate, with the neatest municipal tip in the universe, and then Llanbadarn Fawr. You'll come back to all these places later.

Go down Llanbadarn Road, with its colonial-style mansions, at the end of which you'll be at the bottom of Penglais Hill. Turn left at Y Cŵps, and there's the town. You're on Northgate Street, often locally reviled because of its frequently boarded-up shop fronts but it's home to Hot Dumplings (best hangover-cure food in town) and three wondrous grottoes: Cal Walters's Aber Books and Collectables, Julian Shelley's Second-hand Books and Jewellery, and Andy's Records. All three, superb. I've discovered rare gems in them all (literally so, in Julian's case).

FROM THE SOUTH-EAST: A485

We'll start here from Llanilar, because beyond this your town becomes... well, Aberystwyth again, if you double back on yourself just before Llanafon, beyond which lies typically Ceredigion-esque green swells and bulges like a vast fossilised sea with nothing but small and scattered settlements until the town of Tregaron is reached (fascinating place, but well out of my bailiwick). The road joins the A4120 from Devil's Bridge at Rhydyfelin which, to be honest, is a far more interesting highway, with its ringingly Biblical names (Moriah, Pisgah) and wind-stripped hillocks and deep valleys white-flecked with cottages and sheep. Travelling this road at night-time into Aberystwyth is interesting; from the road above the industrial estate at Glan yr Afon, the town again can look like a city, with the illuminated warehouses and yard lights creating the impression of a larger municipal area and with the bulbs of streetlight and stairwell and underpass making the Penparcau flats seem much taller than they actually are. You can, if you want to, at Llanfarian, join the A487 southern coast road and stop at the Royal Oak there for a pint and wonder who Farian was and, when home, scour the web and your reference shelves for any mention of why s/he was beatified and then realize quickly that you've reached a dead-end and then shrug and then reason that this is mid-Wales, after all, land of ten thousand saints, many of them unknown to the prevailing orthodoxy. After Llanfarian – where the great Saunders Lewis lived between 1937 and

1952 – you can, at Rhydyfelin, take a left towards Morfa Bychan holiday park and explore the coastal path there; get intrepid with the bracken and you might discover small caves in the cliffs, anchorites' cells, or you can keep walking north towards the tall phallic thing on the hill with the sea far below to your left until you find yourself on the top of Allt Wen with the old harbour below you and the Pen Dinas monument directly opposite, at your eye level. Or you can ignore this suggestion and drive down and up through Rhydyfelin, past the turning for Nanteos mansion (where you'll be close enough to hear the ghostly wailing and see the earthlights hovering) and into Penparcau, where you shouldn't stop or even wind your windows down or unlock your doors because this is a big council estate and here they'll boil your head for cawl. You could turn right here, into Llanbadarn, over the Rheidol river, but you should just for the moment carry straight on towards the sea all prettily a-glitter (or, more likely, darkly scowling in drizzle), past another holiday park on your right, and into Trefechan. Londis, fire station, pub, derelict brewery which bears the graffiti *'na i'r mewnlifiad'* ('no incomers'). There's a road here that will take you to the beach, via Pen yr Angor, or another road to the harbour. Offices have been erected here, many of them empty. There's a lime kiln; Worthington's atmospheric painting 'Harbour Aberystwyth'[13] shows this in use; burping black smoke, dark and sooty, heavily industrial. It's not like that anymore. Ahead of you is the Trefechan Bridge, where the modern manifestation of Cymdeithas yr Iaith was born in the 1960s, and that will take you over the Rheidol and into town. Perhaps you'd better fortify yourself in The Fountain first. We'll be coming back here shortly anyway.

FROM THE SOUTH: A487

We'll start, here, at Llanon, because beyond that your town becomes Aberaeron[14]. Llanon's a fairly sizeable village; two pubs [15], a Londis, a butcher's, another chippy, garage, school, and a brilliant bakery in an old mill building on the southern outskirts of the village. The place is named after Non, the mother of St. David, who was born at Henfynyw, a little further down the coast. Not much is known about her; she was either a nun at Whitesand Bay who was seduced by a prince called Sant and who then gave birth to David, or she was the daughter of a Pembrokeshire chieftain, who was married to someone called Sant. She settled first in Cornwall (where there's a church to her at Altarnon) and died in Brittany, where her tomb survives at Dircinon (Finisterre). Her Celtic credentials are impeccable. In the middle ages, Cornwall claimed her relics; a chapel from that time and a well of hers can be seen close to the city of St. David's. Her feast day, in Wales, is on March 3rd[16].

This area is one of pure Celtic Welshness. The language remains strong, on this coast road, and the fields above and the steeply rushing dingles below are marked with megaliths and tumuli and monks' cells. Pembrokeshire, here, becomes Ceredigion, and the landscape declares that; the hills cease to roll and start to peak. Small villages lie in their troughs, absorbing damp. It's a stunningly beautiful road to travel along when the sun shines, as it does today; the sea below me, to the left, looks very blue, as if you'd come out of it the same colour after taking a dip. Between Llanon and Llanrhystud there is a long stretch of road along which people who shouldn't be allowed to drive do, very fast; there are many dips in this road, it is not conducive to overtaking (although the local undertakers do good business). I've come to associate it with the shrieking of brakes and stink of burnt rubber and racing heart and the hand-signal for 'wanker' made through the car window. It is lined with huge mansions; what do these people do – or what have they done – to make so much money? I was told by Cynan Jones, author of the fine novella *The Long Dry* (set on a farm in this area during a heat wave) that, in the woods just off this road, behind the giant houses, there is a series of bunkers in which World War Two internees (Germans living in Britain) were kept whilst put to work flattening the land. The strip of land just prior to Plasgwyn mansion is known as Cae Camp ('Field of the Camp'). Behind the two hills that look like a bosom lie the bunkers. Maes Fron Farm[17], where Cynan grew up, had a bunker on one of its fields. The Jones family never went there, but the young Cynan did go into another one, which terrified him (as it did me, on the Wirral; the darkness and the dripping and the confinement, hideous). I'm keen to explore these bunkers today but can't find a way to them which isn't knee-deep in sucking mud, despite the sun. I'll try another day, but there are places in Wales which are perpetually sodden.

Into Llanrhystud. For some reason, the hillsides around this village often sport a kind of graffiti – large letters burnt, or dug, into their grass. 'EMYR IS GAY', once, hugely carved, visible from the air; today, 'PARRY MARRY PADDY', which is much sweeter, but less funny. We park up and go into the café adjoining the Costcutter for

breakfast, which is perfectly decent; beans on toast with bacon on top, brown tea. The parish church is an impressive building, renovated in 2005 at large cost. The Black Lion pub, which also recently underwent extensive renovation, sits on the banks of the Wyre, which the locals see as the border into Gogland (or 'the north', although I would've put it further up, myself – the Mawddwy estuary, perhaps). 'Gogs are like piles', one old feller will inform me later, in the pub; 'if they come down and stay they're a pain in the arse, but if they go back up again they're alright'. Pitched battles between north and south are sometimes fought on the Wyre bridge; so far this year, seven men have lost their lives (just joking).

We watch crows in the field outside the cafe window as we finish our tea. Corvids are ubiquitous in this part of Wales; carrion crows and magpies and jays and jackdaws. Choughs, too, on the sea-cliffs, sometimes. I'd like to see the hooded crow colonise this area; they're intriguing birds, in their executioner's aprons. All crows intrigue me, really; their behaviour baffles because it differs so from that of other birds, it can seem more human than avian. I've been told about, but never actually witnessed, crow courts; a group of birds will encircle a lone bird and chatter excitedly until, as one, they descend on the single bird and tear it to shreds. What crime could a bird possibly commit to warrant such punishment? Do they have a sense of morality, some system of reward and punishment? They've been observed using tools. I've been advised to inform them of a birth or death. I might as well. Strange, strange creatures.

Just outside Llanrhystud, the A44's 'ELVIS' rock has its counterpart. In a layby, on a single freestanding brick wall that is the only remnant of a house that once stood here, '*COFIWCH DRYWERYN*' has been painted. Tryweryn, you'll remember, was the valley in north Wales that was flooded to supply water to the city of Liverpool, at the displacement of an ancient community and the destruction of their houses and farms and chapels. The flooding went ahead despite the protests and petitions, despite the fact that, with a little more expenditure of money and imagination, Liverpool could've easily been irrigated by other, already existing reservoirs. It was a despicable, criminal act of colonialist aggression, and this makeshift monument to it is painfully poignant. Lost homes. Longing. Anger and aching. There has been talk of demolishing the wall, due to Health and Safety regs, of course; it might collapse onto the lorries that often rest in the layby. That'd be another crime, too[18].

These hills I know like I know the contours of my own body. They glow green today. So many different greens. Each leaf turns on its own tender hinge. We pass the Blaenplwyf transmitter, which allows us to watch *Sgorio* as if through a blizzard. Tiny lambs gather at the fences, close to the busy road. They are as white as an American's teeth and the size of cats. The Pen Dinas monument appears. We pass the posh Conrah Hotel which has recently been taken over but I remember a great meal there with some close friends, the barman like the major in Fawlty Towers who made a superb Bloody Mary. We drive down into Llanfarian, where you've already been, and join the queue of traffic backed up all the way from Aberystwyth, this being a wee bit past 9 a.m. In the back window of the Range Rover in front of us is a golden retriever's arse. It looks like the end of a sausage roll. We're forced to look at it as we chug slowly out of Llanfarian and up through Rhydyfelin and through Penparcau and into town.

FROM THE WEST: SEA

In his great book *The Sea Kingdoms*, Alistair Moffat writes:

> To say that the Celts of Britain have a close affinity with the land and the sea is to underplay a near-umbilical connection. The huge skies of the Atlantic shore, the rose and gold of sunsets dying in the west, the bleakness of the land and the majesty of land and sea together pierce

the hearts of those who are born there. Even if they leave, the west never leaves them.

When I'm inland, in whatever country, I'm aware of a gnawing sense of loss. There's a solidity to those places, of a quantity and of a kind I don't want; nothing there acts like water does, unpredictable and untameable. I could never feel at home, never feel found, in a place that's never known the battering of waves. My blood is salty.

Aberystwyth, of course, is a sea-town. Pen Dinas, the castle, the harbour; all built to deal with the sea, to open negotiations with the waves. Every year, a few students die from taunting the water. I remember a deep-sea buoy ripped free of its moorings by a storm and washed up on the north beach, giant jetsam, at the foot of Constitution Hill; a huge thing, house-high, like a spaceship crash-landed (Gwyneth Lewis wrote a poem about it, but you'll get that later). Snorkelling in the waters I discovered a shelf not far from the shore which plunged into deep water and at the slope of which life gathered; blennies, crabs, sprats, even lobsters, blue and slow and dangerous. Dogfish, topes. Exploring the rock pools once I saw a seahorse, his tail wrapped around a seaweed frond; as I watched, he let go of his anchor and see-sawed gently away to hide in a crack in the rock. I read in the paper later that day that short-nosed seahorses were thought by oceanographers to have drifted as far north as mid-Wales; I'd seen the proof that they had. Never have I been so astonished by a creature in all my life. Dreamlike thing. Beautifully preposterous. Another time, the surface of the sea was carpeted with ladybirds; when I surfaced through them, as of course I had to, they squirted my face and neck and shoulders with acid. Very painful. And some years ago, a fishing boat caught a basking shark; the restaurants and fishmongers in the town sold shark steaks for months. I ate one, in a pub. Was unimpressed.

From a boat, the town again looks like a city. From a boat, on a summer's evening, it can look almost Mediterranean; salty and spicy and sexy. 'The air', Mike Parker writes in an email, 'in the fuschia-flooded alleys and back lanes, hangs heavy and sweet, and Aber's lust expresses itself across the boundaries. Welsh, English, resident, visitor, straight, gay, serious, dabbler, who's counting?'

Fires burn on the beach, and the sea-front bars boom. Beyond the lights of the fires, illicit goings-on go on; drugs, whisper it, may be taken; couplings, whisper it, may take place. Mike Parker again, in his *Neighbours from Hell*, quotes from an 1820s English guidebook to

Aberystwyth: 'The lower classes here, as in many other parts of Wales, indiscriminately dress and undress on the sands, and pay very little distinction to their sex'. Brilliant; snobbery, racism, homophobia – three strikes in one sentence. They didn't mess about, those Victorians. Imagine the outraged unravelling of his waxed moustache.

The liminality of sea-towns allows libidinous expression. The uncapturability of water, and the constant presence of that, highlights the porousness of imposed and alien codes of morality. True, chapel strains to staunch such cracks but sea-towns, and the people in them, know all about steady erosion, about how temporary human structures are, how inevitable is the washing away of our stamp, and of how terribly, terribly brief the life of the flesh is.

Another memory: the beach is covered in starfish. Tens of thousands of them. The seagulls come down in a cloud, as do the crows. It's amazing, what the sea decides to jettison. From a boat, the town itself can look like jetsam, thrown up by the waves. Exploring it is simply beachcombing. Aber-based novelist Richard Collins knows this; his *The Land as Viewed from the Sea* is about precisely that – love, betrayal, creativity and destruction – everything that resides at the tide-line.

notes

1. See Dylan Davies (B).
2. Ditto.
3. In *The Confirmation*.
4. 'Lol' = 'nonsense', made adjectival by the 'fa'. I think.
5. See Our Century in 'Works Consulted'.
6. R.S. Thomas's quintessential Welsh shangri-la kind of thing. See his *Selected Prose*.
7. This contains a recipe for beetroot wine, a batch of which I made in 2000. I'm still drunk.
8. *My Kingdom of Books*, Y Lolfa, 1999. Richard Booth declared Hay-on-Wye as an independent state and himself as its crowned king. He effectively turned it from a small borders market town into the metropolis of second-hand books and festivals that it is today.
9. Except it's now been solved, or at least partly. Mike Parker, in an episode of his BBC Wales series *Great Welsh Roads*, interviewed a couple of older fellers who admitted to painting the rock in the 60s as part of their canvassing for Islwyn Ffowc Elis, except they mis-spelled the surname with two 'l's. That night, a person or persons unknown turned one of the 'l's into a 'v'. So the mystery is over. But neither 'l' looks like it was ever a 'v'. And who was the unknown vandal of the vandalism? It doesn't matter, really. The 'ELVIS' rock has been a Pumlumon landmark for over 40 years and long may it stay so.
10. See Stallion's Crag.
11. Patty Duncker again, from a personal email: 'the phenomenon that intrigued me was the fact that Aber's micro-climate... can sometimes be left behind with DRAMATIC suddenness

– just rise up the hill and it's as cold as November in May and all around there is nothing but rain and mist'.

12. See *Wild Wales*.
13. Reproduced on the cover of J. Geraint Jenkins's *Ceredigion*.
14. Which is a great wee place; ducks and pubs and, in the Celtic, the best chipshop in Ceredigion. What more could you want? Well, many things, but that's enough for a small happiness.
15. In one of which I got felt up, late at night, by a drunken middle-aged man. Before I ran away he told me he'd lost his wife. Can't imagine in what ways I was any kind of a substitute for her.
16. See Farmer in 'Works Consulted'.
17. 'Fron' is a mutation of 'Bron', another Welsh word for 'hill', specifically a hill that resembles a woman's breast. It's a beautiful language.
18. There's a lot more to be said about the Tryweryn drowning, and I'll do so in *Real Liverpool*, forthcoming. But others have discussed it powerfully and eloquently already.

OUTSKIRTS

TREFECHAN/PEN YR ANGOR

From the south beach, or Tan y Bwlch – the 'gap of fire', and the weird sculptures of volcanic rock here point to the historic flavour of Welsh nomenclature – you can see reminders of three wars; the Wellington monument atop Pen Dinas, and the concrete pillbox from World War Two, just over the bridge that spans the Rheidol where it meets the sea and on which cats gather, scowling and rapacious and serious, whenever sea-bass chase sprats up onto the shingle. The marshy plain to the right of Pen Dinas used to be a landfill site, but isn't anymore, and the semi-detached cottages which cling precariously to the crumbling bank used to be (or so I've been told) a hospital for shell-shocked veterans of World War One, and then a TB sanatorium. What they're used for now, I don't know. Just more of those lost buildings in this town, the purpose and provenance of which is hidden (although I'll probably discover that their function is a lot more prosaic, now, than I'd like). Herons sometimes stalk this river. Marram grass and sea-pinks spot with colour the Rheidol's running sides. Outdoor parties were once held here; again, not any more, unless of course I've missed them. This place is close enough to the town to hear the town's noise, but distant enough to feel isolate; it's a pleasant place to laze away a summer's day, the sea-cliffs disappearing to the south in the heat haze, as if they're really vanishing, becoming unmade. The current and steep tidal shelf here ensure that the waves never lap but launch themselves up to smash on the shingle; a furious sound that can strangely soothe.

The pillbox isn't worth exploring, unless you like crouching in

cramped darkness amongst garbage in the stink of stale piss (well, some people do). Pen yr Angor itself has the feel of a remote country lane, although that tang is becoming weaker each year with the increasing levels of housing going up at this desirable spot. The relatively recent (and horribly expensive) harbour flats now block the sea-view of the houses that occupy the lower slopes of Pen Dinas; one man's boosted equity is another's restricted amenity. So it goes. Cottages housed the dock workers, here, when Aber had a functioning dock; few of those cottages remain, and none of the workers. The Aber-Carmarthen railway would begin here, loaded with coal or timber; now, the fire station sits on the site of one of two huge timber-yards that used to be here. And if you can see the fire station then you're in Trefechan, or 'Turkey', as it used to be known.

Herbert Williams, the writer, was born here, in Turkey, on Glan yr Afon Terrace, 74 years ago. He's now lived in Cardiff for many years but he remembers Turkey as being the rough part of town. Why Trefechan became Turkey, he doesn't know; one of those remote connections that port towns, however small, tend to make. Will Troughton's *Aberystwyth Voices* collects in its last chapter recollections of Turkey; these voices talk of fights between here and Tan y Cae, or South Road; 'always stone fights and rough. The football team used to win the cup and were noted for roughness'. At one time, there were six pubs here; now there's just one, The Fountain, which I'm fond of. It's dark and safe and lively and keeps its beer well. Plus it has a fish tank. 'Trefechan', of course, means 'little town', and it's not really that anymore; a general store, a pet shop and a pub do not really make for exhaustive municipal services. The brewery now is a derelict shell bearing the sprayed-on words '*NA I'R MEWNLIFIAD*',[1] which you'll read as you leave the town. But it has its beginnings as an ancient little settlement; 'the materials for the building of the castle were unloaded here', as W.J. Lewis writes[2]: 'Aberystwyth's industrial suburb, [Trefechan] has housed boat and shipbuilding yards, six lime kilns, a hop drying kiln, maltsters, a lead smeltery, timber yards, a cooperage,

brickworks, several smithies... a ropeyard, two sail lofts, a foundry and a brewery'. It also had two doss houses, where tramps could get a bed and a meal for half a pence. These were often skilled men who'd simply had a run of bad luck; 'it is said that when solicitors were short of someone who could write in good copperplate style, the doss house would often produce the right person'. The hop house is now a recording

studio. Or was, up until very recently.

So I speak to Herb in a place I very much like. Old maps show it to be separate from Aberystwyth at one time, even with the umbilicus of the bridge, and it still retains something of that feeling. We meet in the castle grounds in the early afternoon and go to the Castle pub, which is closed, so we walk over the bridge and into Trefechan, where we try The Fountain. Also closed. So we buy sandwiches and crisps and bottled water from the general store next door and sit on a bench opposite, by the fire station. There's a wind blowing. The sea-smell today is unusually strong. Itchy ozone in the nostrils.

Herb's been around long enough to be a living link to a world gone. He contracted TB here, in Trefechan, at the age of sixteen, and had to wait five months to get a bed in a sanatorium near Brecon: 'It was like trying to get into Eton in them days,' he says. He writes about this in his novel *A Severe Case of Dandruff*. He was there two years.

Everyone who passes says hello to Herb. It's as if he never left the town. His upbringing was remarkable; eight people in a three bedroomed house, no running water, no bathroom. There was 'a terrible curse of illness', and his brother Bobby died at twenty-five, but there was also 'a great intellectual drive in the house', and, while Turkey's fights went on outside, Herb would find a quiet place in the house and read. The teetotalism of both his parents was probably a blessing, and ensured Herb's long and, after his recovery from TB, healthy life. He remembers, as a child, walking with his mother up Bridge Street, past the Llew Du pub, which he thought was advertising a 'free house', a solution to the overcrowding at home. He excitedly pointed this out to his mother who told him never to set foot in such places. But the brewery, and the nearby Corona factory[3] supplied much work to the locals; 'the thud of beer barrels and the tinkling of pop bottles[4] was quite musical in it's way,' Herb says.

His novel *The Woman in Back Row*, which features Aberystwyth in the guise of Glenaber, is based on his days as a reporter for the *Welsh Gazette*, which was the rural paper to the *Cambrian News*'s town one. His column was his apprenticeship as a writer. He left Aber in 1956 at age twenty-four, with his wife Dorothy, to whom he's still married. He has five children, nine grandchildren, and two great-grandchildren. He still writes. At some point in our conversation he refers to Wynford Vaughan Thomas, another Aber resident, who once said that 'Aberystwyth is the perfect town for the unambitious man'.

We both laugh at this. As we do, a biker drives past, music blaring from his machine. How can he hear it, through his full-face helmet?

I have to admire his ambition.

The Pen Dinas hill fort looms over Trefechan, and Herb and I, on our bench. Like any other large swell of land in Wales, the people who live at its foot – and how could they not, in a small yet mountainous country? – seem both shrivelled and augmented by its presence. Herb wrote about this in his fine poem 'Hill Fort':

> I spy them often, crouching
> on the terraces, small,
> restless men, watchful as thieves.
>
> Their eyes are sharp, missing
> only the things that I can see,
> roofs on the lower slopes,
> the lean white arms
> of a wind farm in the distance.
>
> They see
> what they have always seen,
> a world where every
> lesson has been learned
> and safety lies
> in high, green places.
>
> Valleys floors
> are best avoided.
> Shades of a future
> where there's no safety at all.

That's a part of living in Wales; the valley floor settlements have been built in shadow. Eyes are always tugged upwards, to the uplands. Sun spills from them; rain, too. A different climate abuts people's lives.

Trefechan's bridge, that spans the Rheidol into the town proper, has taken on an iconic significance in contemporary Welsh politics. The original structure probably trembled under the plod of mammoths but in 1800 John Nash designed one, at a cost of £1,402 (there are several beautiful paintings of this in The Coliseum). This was destroyed by flood in 1886 and replaced by the present one, built by David Lloyd to a design by the wonderfully-named Sir James Szlumper. It's an elegant, impressive piece of engineering, wind-swept perpetually. On 13th February 1963, Cymdeithas yr Iaith Gymraeg (the Welsh Language Society) members blocked the bridge, stopping traffic for half an hour, in protest at the lowly status of the Welsh language in bureaucratic dealings and an unfair housing policy. Hardly a spectacular act, but it's repercussions reached far. It was a catalyst. Dafydd Iwan sang:

> Do you remember Trefechan Bridge
> And the first ever protest
> And the Cardis couldn't understand
> Why the Welshies were blocking their street?

Which points to the atomisation of the Welsh identity at the time which was, to an extent, re-dressed by the Trefechan event. Carwyn Fowler's and Rhys Jones's essay 'Crud Cenedlaetholdeb Cymreig' ('Cradle of Welsh Nationalism') came out of their commissioned research (by the University of Wales Board of Celtic Studies) into the growth of Welsh nationalism in Aberystwyth, how it runs like a vein throughout the town's mortar and memory and current sense of self. It begins with the 'accident' of Trefechan Bridge; the idea was to protest at the Post Office, in a nod to the Dublin Easter Rising, and effect arrests so that the protestors (who included Tegwyn Jones, Tedi Millward, Geraint Jones and John Davies – luminaries all), after the Pen-y-Berth Three (more on whom later), could draw attention to their aims and grievances in a public arena. There was no police presence at the P.O., however, so the group adjourned to the Home

Café, where some of them (there was a schism) decided to block Trefechan Bridge. And so a kind of history was made. There is a plaque on the bridge today commemorating that morning, 'though it says', to quote John Davies (from Fowler's and Jones's essay), 'a little unfortunately, that this was Cymdeithas yr Iaith Gymraeg's first 'non-violent protest', as if there had been some history of violent protests before that. The wording is a bit unfortunate to say the least'. Fair point. But when a status quo – that is, when an unfair and assiduously self-serving judicial and civic apparatus – is smashed, it feels like a kind of violence has been done; largely to property, of course, but also to the rigid mindsets of those who make and sustain and support those laws. This is no bad thing. There should be more of it.

But John Davies is of course right to point out that any political protest is marred with the taint of 'violence' and used in that way to undermine sympathy and support.

So the bridge at Trefechan has become a metaphorical span, too, between Cymro-Wales and Anglo-Wales, between Welsh identity pre- and post-1963. It doesn't just link Trefechan with the town; it links the town with the rest of Wales, the nascent nation-state (maybe...) and thus the whole of Europe. Ned Thomas, however, author of, amongst other things, *The Welsh Extremist*, told me that the notion of Cymdeithas yr Iaith beginning in Trefechan is a myth, and that its real birth occurred some years later, with the switching off of the Pencarreg transmitter. This was at the height of the broadcasting campaign, when Ned was on the senate of Cymdeithas yr Iaith. He calls it, with a bit of a tongue-in-cheek twinkle, his 'moment of militant glory', when Willie Whitelaw reneged on his promise to establish a Welsh-language TV station, so Ned and Meredith Evans and Pennar Davies turned off the transmitter. They were charged with burglary[5], and fined £1,000, but this money had already been collected at that year's eisteddfod. Still the TV station didn't materialise, until Gwynfor Evans threatened hunger strike.

We'll spend more time with these people later. For the moment, look north, to the big grey bulk of the National Library. Behind that is the university's newer campus. And behind that is Waunfawr.

WAUNFAWR

'Waunfawr' means 'big moor', and that's kind of what it is; little grass here now visible beneath or between the houses but the large estate of modern, low housing is a featureless plain of another sort. There's a Co-op, a Spar, a chippy, and a secondary school[6], but mostly there's just houses, all similar, built along wide boulevards and culs-de-sac, each with a garage and a patch of garden. It's just suburbia, akin to the large estates that outlie all towns and cities in the British Isles. Were it not for the Welsh street-signs, you could be outside Exeter. Or Carlisle. Or Walsall. Or anywhere.

The poet Paul Henry was brought up here, in Maeshendre. He lives in Newport now. He emailed me a photograph of Waunfawr Wanderers, taken during the 1970-71 season; thirteen boys in oversized strip, huddled together against the cold, cuffs pulled over their fingers. One of them went on to play for Tranmere Rovers and Wrexham; another, to lose his mind and throw himself under a train. It's a sad photograph, as its kind always is. Paul's accompanying letter enlivens it somewhat; 'I think', he writes, 'I was lucky to be a young child [in Aber], at a time when monochrome turned to colour, to psychedelic colour – a unique time perhaps: 'bible-black' elders puzzling at my sister's gang in The Cabin, in their bright miniskirts – all that colour come to a grey town'. The photograph is monochrome, but the red and black stripes of the boys' AC Milan shirts can be discerned; their kit was supplied by Jimmy Antoniazzi, who ran The Penguin Cafe at the top of Bridge Street. AC must've been his team. After he kitted them out, Waunfawr Wanderers started winning, playing on a patch of marshland called 'The Bog', next to where the Co-op now stands.

Paul's poetry is soaked with loss, with unrecoverable memories, and is concomitantly saddened and outraged at the passage of time. His poem 'Maeshendre'[7], in it's entirety, reads: 'A rush of small soles on the pavement/passes and is gone./A bustle of wings takes off'. It is quiet, moving, reflective work. 'Marine Terrace'[8] records the ways in which the town of Paul's birth has changed:

> Inside The Cabin, a new breath blows
> the surf from the cappuccinos
>
> and where the stonemason's was
> Westcoast Tattoo's moved in

so we grieve them by this rose
on a thigh, this buttock's butterfly,

our town's unfashionable dead.

I like Westcoast Tattoo; they put the snake on my girlfriend's back, and took over the small free-standing building that was once occupied by the unfriendliest record shop in the entire country (the very opposite to Andy's, a couple of hundred yards down the road, and Backbeat, around the corner, facing the train station). But, although Aberystwyth's in my childhood, my childhood's not in Aberystwyth, and Paul's poetry is as poignantly evocative as the old postcards and photographs that his good friend Will Troughton collects in their thousands. Frozen instants; a momentary catching of the quick which often tells more of the dead. 'Time's a shell of the snail it was', Paul writes. And it is.

LLANBADARN FAWR

In many ways – historical, spiritual, ecumenical – Llanbadarn Fawr is just as, if not more important than, Aberystwyth itself, a scant two miles away to the west. Its saint – Padarn, or Paternus of Wales – founded the church here 'of which he was both Abbot and bishop for twenty years and from which he evangelized the neighbouring countryside'[9]. Giraldus Cambrensis – who doesn't even mention Aberystwyth in his *Journey Through Wales* – made a pilgrimage there in 1188 and discovered a scandal:

> this church... has a layman as what is called its Abbott. There has come a lamentable use and custom by which the most powerful people in a parish have been appointed by the clergy as stewards in the first place [and] in the process of time their greed has grown greater and they have usurped full power, in their impudence appropriating all church lands and assuming secular possession, leaving to the clergy nothing but their altars.... These so-called defenders of the churches, who are really bent on destroying what they should protect, have taken the name of abbotts, presuming to attribute tothemselves not only a title but also lands to which they have no right. We found the church at Llanbadarn Fawr reduced to this sorry state.

Hypocrisy, gerrymandering, nepotism, greed; the same things

stoked Caradoc Evans's fury six centuries later (although, of course, he didn't agree with Gerald's further point that the Welsh church was better off answering to England). Dafydd ap Gwilym wrote one of his most celebrated poems about the church here, although he was more interested in the comeliness of the women in it than of the building itself:

> No Sunday ever was there in Llanbadarn
> that I would not be – and others will condemn it –
> facing some such lovely girl
> with my nape to God's true loveliness[10]

The *Rough Guide to Wales*, by Mike Parker and Paul Whitfield – a constantly reliable guide to all things bright and naughty – calls the church a 'stunning sight', which it is, and lists its attractions; the dizzyingly sloping graveyard; the enlargement of a page from Rhygyfarch's *Psalter* of 1079, hanging just inside the church door; and, most spectacularly, the two tenth century stone crosses in the south transept exhibition, moved inside from the graveyard during the First World War. They're beautiful, these crosses; touch them, and the iciness in their stone prickles your marrow; they seem, almost, to thrum in your hand. The taller one is 'woven with exquisite Celtic tracery', to quote the *Rough Guide*. I lived in Llanbadarn, when I first moved to the area, and visited the church a lot, and, in the summer, would take a book and a bag of apples up into the steep cemetery. Peaceful times amongst the dead, who often have an awful lot to say for themselves, but didn't then. On my last visit to the real thing, it

had an exhibition by Christian Aid exhorting us to 'hold UK companies accountable for their actions overseas'. 'We believe in life before death' is the motto on the pamphlet, and 'keep making poverty history', which is, of course, a laudable aim, but one that I fear will remain unreachable unless we make obscene wealth history first. The *Pobl Dewi* diocese newspaper I picked up carried discussions between those of Christian and Muslim faiths, and the single sheet of information produced by the Penglais School History Society is crammed with interesting gems: 'St. Padarn persuaded a local chieftain, Maelgwyn Gwynedd, to give him all the land between the rivers Rheidol and Clarach to establish a monastery. As the Celtic church is proud to recall this took place *before* St. Augustine's mission to the  English in 597' (their italics). Terrific. It goes on to list the inscriptions on the church bells. It's a great piece of compressed data, this single badly-xeroxed sheet. The History Society of Penglais School clearly know their stuff.

And there's more to Llanbadarn than the church, lovely though that is. When I lived there, there were two general stores, a chippy, a post office, and a launderette; these have now gone, but the garage shop has expanded into a mini-market and the huge Morrisons supermarket at Parc-y-Llyn is within walking distance (as they often are). There is a vet's, which holds sad memories; my pet rat was put down in there. Tumours. He was three, which is old for a domestic rat. As the injected chemical took effect, he appeared to panic, and dragged his broken body across the table and into my hand where he curled up and died. He was a good companion; he'd often sleep on my chest as I, in turn, slept. Two pubs still exist in Llanbadarn; the Black Lion and the Gogerddan Arms, on opposite sides of the square, the war memorial between them. The low wall surrounding that monument contains Y Garreg Fawr, a capstone that once was part of a much larger structure (probably a burial chamber) which belonged to the Powells of Nanteos in their office of Lords of the Manor of Llanbadarn Fawr, and from which, during the Civil Wars, 'more extreme sects and preachers such as Vavasor Powell and Richard Davies preached rousing sermons'[11]. The Modern Antiquarian website dispatched a field operative there in 2002. S/he writes:

> Back in 1867 a gentleman called Mr Morgan wrote about Garreg Fawr.... He describes how it once 'stood on pillars of the same material'

but was 'fractured by the kindling of a bonfire upon it'. Before its destruction the tomb appears to have been the focal point for village life. Morgan says that 'the [village] crier used to proclaim all matters of public interest' from the monument.

Not particularly informative, no, but it's interesting the way these pre-Christian artefacts have been absorbed into general diurnality in these parts; you can lean against this capstone as you read the roll of the dead on the war memorial. The grand crosses in the church might also have been pagan standing stones; an act of Gravesian iconotropy[12] which, for once, has resulted in a new beauty.

I take a few snaps of the capstone and go to meet Matt Jarvis in the Black Lion. Matt's a writer and lecturer at the university, Birmingham-born, doctor in modern British poetry, been living in Aber since 1994. He's the author of 'An Aberystwyth Canto' (see the 'Harbour' section) and has a novel in progress set in a small Welsh seaside town with a university. The twelve years he's lived in Aber are the longest he's lived anywhere; 'Aber is a space in which romance can happen as well as history', he says, 'with the wind coming in off the sea.... It's an easy place to be at home in, and that's speaking as an Englishman. This town is where I became an adult'. He's always felt welcome, he says, either in the town centre or in Llanbadarn, and has found no real problem of access to either linguistic community. Downsides? 'Well, employment is bad and house prices are high. But I'm emotionally wedded to the place like nowhere else I've been.' He tells me that he misses having stories passed down, as through his parents, to do with the place in which they live, but he's gathering his

own stories and now passing them down to his young son, and thus establishing that connective oral and emotional history that, like most writers, he finds so valuable. This is a place in which to do that; Aberystwyth's floors bulge and buckle with the strength of the roots that people sink. Births of dynasties.

Around the corner from the Black Lion, on the road out towards Goginan and built slightly up from that road, stands Father's House. This was a drug and alcohol rehab centre which received £300,000 lottery money in 2002 but closed in 2006. The *Cambrian News* called this a 'debacle'[13]. One of the trustees, the Reverend Geoffrey Thomas, was quoted as saying: 'We tried for more government funding, but the scheme was heavily over-subsidised, and Father's House closed down. About 200 men passed through it and alcohol and drug programmes were offered. Some wouldn't take help, but a number did. One of the weaknesses was that the trustees were not hands-on enough. There was a feeling of sadness that it had closed'.

Indeed, the scheme began with a wrong decision, the awarding of a major grant to a group of people 'who admitted they had no track record in the field of substance-misuse counselling'[14]. A presentation was made to Father's House in 1998 by Keith Hellawell, the so-called drugs czar[15]. At the time, there was an established rehab centre in Rhoserchan at Capel Seion, just a few miles away, which had applied for funding to no avail. This, too, closed.

When asked about this affair, my contacts at Community Safety Partnership and related organisations throw their hands up in exasperated despair and point me to statistics which only prove that Aber desperately needs a working and centred rehabilitation service. An Alcohol Development Worker who I meet in The Cabin on Pier Street one sun-soaked July afternoon tells me about the local drinking dynasties – how all the names of those in the nearby clinics are connected somehow, by blood, marriage, or simply an event. Alcohol runs through the town like a third river. As does chapel; one side of a family might be teetotal, the other side severely alcoholic. My contact – let's call him Steve, because that's not his name – is very aware of the ambiguities of language and he uses words very carefully, always attentive to how they can be misconstrued by the aggressively paranoid, those keen to look for slight and slur, some specific thing on which to pin their pain. He says that he supplies a 'cognitive service'; he teaches people to re-frame their thinking, to examine and modify their behaviour. But he needs somewhere safe and discreet in which to do that, which, at the moment, he doesn't have[16].

At the time of writing, another rehab centre is being prepared for opening, but obviously I can't say where that is. Cambrian Street has a night shelter, and the Walich Clifford Community Centre on Chalybeate Street have opened a re-settlement facility in the town. So things are being done to assist the lost and the lonely, the damaged and the damaging. But I wonder, as always, why that isn't the first item on everyone's agenda; why it far too frequently feels like someone's after-thought. Steve can only work with the tools he's allowed to use.

Anyway. Leave Llanbadarn via the Quebec Road, and feel the echoes of the *Good Brig Credo* as you do. Quebec Road becomes Llanbadarn Road at the water trough, opposite the car-dealership, by the new roundabout, about half way down. This will take you into town.

COMINS COCH

Comins Coch – the 'red common' – is a suburb of Aber built on top of the hill between the university and the hamlet of Capel Dewi. It was probably, once, a wee, self-contained village, but now it's really overspill; two large estates built in the last forty years have bled the place into Waunfawr. It has no pub, or shop (although the Co-op is within walking distance), but John Barnie, who lives there, tells me that his house was once 'a sort of shop, with tins of salmon and so on'. He emails me that Comins 'is still slightly more than a mere dormitory extension of Aber', and fleshes out the place for me, explaining that the village contains two distinct social groupings, 'one based on the council estate, working-class, a mix of Welsh and English incomers; [and] the Trefaenor estate of semi-detached houses built in the 1980s, same linguistic mixture, but more middle-class'. He writes that 'the Welsh speakers and the English only mix very superficially, which, in my opinion, makes Comins rather different to many of Aber's outlying villages, and that 'the English residents have absolutely no idea of the range of cultural activity going on in Welsh', which makes it the same.

If you're at all interested in Aberystwyth, or know anything about it, then you probably know who John Barnie is; writer, journalist, musician, and, of course, editor of *Planet* (until his recent retire-ment), whose offices are on the Science Park, that cluster of Scandinavian-looking buildings just off the vertiginously steep Cefn Llan which connects the Waun to Llanbadarn. John's originally from Abergavenny, a town of similar size to Aberystwyth, and came here in 1985 to work as assistant editor on the re-launch of *Planet*, which was re-located here from Llangeitho by Ned Thomas, its editor and founder, who you'll meet in a few pages. John's somewhat in thrall to Aberystwyth; his email goes on to say that

> Aber has layers on layers, and what makes it unique is the fact that, while it has all the small-town qualities I feel at home with, it has an

amazingly rich cultural/intellectual life as well. I don't know of a town of a similar size that has a university, houses a National Library, is home to magazines like the *New Welsh Review* and *Planet*, with publishers like Honno[17], Y Lolfa and Gwasg Gomer [nearby]. Then there's the Arts Centre, one of the best in Wales. In what other town of it's size can you go down to a pub like Y Cŵps and meet writers, historians, language activists, or attend a lecture series in Yr Hen Coleg, or go to a concert... by blues giants like David Honeyboy Edwards?

He's right, of course; Aber's cultural richness is one of the town's attractions, and, for most who stay, a reason for doing so. John Barnie, like Ned Thomas, is one of those residents who augments that richness, and who runs through the town's cultural life like a leitmotif. On Aber's Welshness, John writes that he 'enjoys the vibrancy of a town with two languages.... I enjoy this sneaking out of one language and into another, and the glimpse it gives to an outsider of what is the deepest cultural layer of the town'. On this, and on the history of *Planet*, he exhorted me to contact Ned Thomas. So I did. Wait a bit.

Lucy Gough also lives in Comins Coch. Well, not really – she lives between there and Capel Dewi on a road that I'm sure will soon be incorporated into Comins as the estates there spread and expand. She's a playwright for both stage and radio and, startlingly, a grandmother. Until very recently, she made a (very good) living writing for Channel 4's *Hollyoaks*, but she's given that up, after a decade, 'due to boredom'. She was born in London, but brought up in Beddgelert and Fishguard, after which she moved to Aber, with two small children, to study drama. That was over twenty years ago.

We meet up in the caff of Arthur Newman's garden centre, amongst the sweet smell of flowers and the tinkling of the water features and the chirruping of the caged birds. We drink tea. I ask her if Aber's in her work – in her scores of plays – and she replies: 'Not really.... It's my sanctuary from the urban nightmares in my writing'. But the sea is ever-present in her work, as are mountains; *The Raft* imagines cold turkey as a descent into briny hell. Her take on Aber is that 'it's more eccentric than anarchic'; every day she can 'walk around a corner of a street and it feels different to me. I don't think that's due to Alzheimer's'. One of her earliest memories of the place is of walking down Cambrian Street and hearing Brith Gof theatre company loudly rehearsing in the Barn Centre there (where *Planet* also had offices[18], long since demolished for flats). 'The place had such a creative buzz'.

Aber is a sanctuary to her: 'I can do all the strange travelling in my head from a place where I feel physically safe'.

Nondescript Comins, then, bubbling with all this. A line from Lucy's *By a Thread* reads: 'You're making pretty pictures out of misery'. Not to suggest that Comins is in any way miserable, or at least not to any greater degree than any other place where humans might gather and interact, you understand. It's just a good line, that's all.

PENPARCAU

Wild west. Lawless lands. Bandit country. You're in Aber's Toxteth, Brixton, Chapeltown, St. Paul's. Drunken berserkers rage and boil on every street corner. Crack is smoked in the underpass. Get out of here before you're mugged or buggered or both or worse.

Not really, of course; reputations are always exaggerated. Each of the three big estates that make up Penparcau have their share of people with problems, more so than in any other part of the town perhaps, but there's also well-tended lawns and clean cars and cheery service in the Spar or the take-aways or the Co-op (yes, another one). There's a school and a hall and the ubiquitous chapels and a playing field and a stretch of allotments abutting the banks of the Rheidol at the foot of the hill that leads into Llanbadarn Fawr[19]. There's Bodlondeb, the old people's home. There are some great views over the town. The Pen Dinas hill and monument tower over it all. A playground across which crows hop. Red kites sometimes perch on the roofs or lampposts.

All the same, it's not the kind of place one should hang around with a camera, really, and I feel conspicuous and disrespectful, taking my snaps. The Tollgate pub is a peculiar building, as is the crumbling Catholic church adjacent, the sign outside of which – hand painted and amateurish – reads EGLWYS CATHOLIC/ MERTHYRION CYMRU. I wonder which martyrs it's referring to, exactly? Could be any of thousands. Intriguing. A footpath past this will take you up to the Wellington monument atop Pen Dinas, overlooking the sea.... Typical Aberystwyth; within spitting distance of these large estates and you could be on Strumble Head or the Llŷn.

Housing is cheap (ish) in Penparcau, especially in the flats, which accounts partly for the relatively high levels of activity here in which the Dyfed-Powys constabulary might profess an interest. But prices are rising even here. Michel Foucault, in his *Discipline and Punish* (I think; definitely somewhere, anyway), remarked on the particular planning of estates; wide culs-de-sac and boulevards, he said, were easily watchable and thus easily policeable. Personal space and privacy are not factored in to the blueprints. That's noticeable in most new estates but not, for some reason, in Penparcau; here there are blind alleys and ginnels and myriad connecting passages. They're warrens. I don't know whether that's down to faith in the improvability of human nature or a lack of foresight on behalf of the municipal architects. Either way, I know many people who are thankful for the lay-out. I can't blame them.

There's a caravan park between the estates and Trefechan to which English visitors often ask directions. Their pronunciation is remarkable; 'it's by that place', they say, and ask me if there's a writing implement for each bovine animal.

NANTEOS AND THE HOLY GRAIL

Within a flick of a fag butt of the Penparcau estates is Nanteos mansion. On the A485 heading south, opposite the hotel, a small road – the B4340, to Trawsgoed – branches off from the Devil's Bridge road and this will take you to Nanteos. Follow the signs; take some binoculars so you can see them, tiny as they are. There's a wild feeling to this road, and a watery one, too, skirting as it does a lake and a stream and with rain dripping off the overhanging branches. We see rabbits. Squabbling magpies. Ramshackle outhouses and Romany-style caravans surround the imposing mansion which is dark and quiet and closed, although a sign on the door tells us we are welcome to explore the grounds. Wind and cows. A scattering of rusted vehicles around the back of the stable yard in which I used to go to many parties. There's a strange, good feeling to the place. Alluring, is the word. Green fields rise up to a treed ridge and dark woods seem to shuffle closer whenever I look away.

The house itself is now a B & B. Legends surround it, not the least of which being that it houses the Holy Grail. It lies in the Paith Valley and was built on the Neuadd Llawdden and first occupied by Colonel John Jones, who raised the Cardiganshire Militia in support of King Charles I during the Civil War[20]. It passed, via marriage, to the ownership of William Powell, who was the only son of Thomas Powell, one of King James II's knights, and then to his progeny, one of whom, George, when presented with a shotgun by his father, William Thomas Rowland Powell, immediately blasted the life out of his dad's prize bull. William Thomas liked to direct, from his wheelchair, pitch battles on the lawns in front of the mansion; servants and tenants and locals would, at his urging, wage war on each other. How violent these fights got isn't recorded. William Thomas's son, George, befriended the poet Algernon Swinburne, and was invited to dine with Wagner in 1876. He tried to establish a free library and art gallery in Aberystwyth but died, at forty, before this could happen.

And so on. More marriages, more deaths. Fading grandeur became the measure. Margaret, wife of Edward Powell, started an affair with Lord Ystwyth of Tan y Bwlch. When Edward was away or

drunk, she'd raise a bed sheet from a flagpole on the roof of the mansion and Lord Ystwyth would come a-scampering. All the Powells are buried in Llanbadarn churchyard; Edward's and Margaret's bones moulder in the same unmarked grave as William Beauclerk's and Anna Maria Powell's. All jumbled up together. As in life. Edward was the end of the male line at Nanteos and when he died,

Margaret bequeathed the place to a distant relation, Elizabeth Mirylees. Who sold up eleven years later. More changes of ownership. More creeping dereliction.

It's a grand building, all the same. Sixty-nine rooms. Bullet holes in the fireplace marble and a peephole in the bathroom. The stable yard is also impressive, built to a Romanesque design by Cockerill. The walled garden comprises four acres, although the greenhouses and vinery are in a ruinous state. The pet cemetery dates back to 1865; buried there are 'Poor Jack the coon and Jenny his wife', amongst others.

And then there's the Holy Grail. A carved wooden remnant of an old drinking vessel was brought to the mansion by seven monks from Strata Florida on the dissolution of that abbey under Henry VIII and it remained there after their several deaths. Its healing powers became known. Apparently, it's made of olive wood or wych elm and origi-nally measured 12 cm by 12 cm although a lot of it has been nibbled away by the teeth of the dying or the desperate and it now measures 10 cm by 8.5 cm. It doesn't always reside at Nanteos, and Byron Rogers 'almost' found it at Lloyds Bank in Aberystwyth[21]. His essay about his search for *Y Graal Sanctaidd* points to the plausibility of the story, if not to the actuality of the object itself, and certainly to the possibility of it ending up in Nanteos, 'like part of a coconut shell with teeth marks on it'. Aggressive interest from American funda-mentalist churches forced the Grail into peripatetism in the early 1960s. Rogers talks about a man who drank from it after suffering a stroke and declared: 'I may not believe that it is from the Last Supper, but when so many people have believed in something for so long, that thing acquires power', and Rogers himself decanted some water from it into a bottle which he now treats 'with the wariness I reserve for fuse boxes'.

So do fetishes acquire their status, not just to enthrall, but to disap-point, too. The Book of Thoth website has an account of a quest to Nanteos, a 'Grade 1 listed, 18th century Palladian mansion that is a starless bed and breakfast'. The writer has dug up some dirt on

George Powell; 'a masochistic homosexual with a fondness for the birch and the works of the Marquis de Sade'. He is shown round the place by its resident caretaker and sole tenant, an ageing hippy who wants to show him the top floor 'because the Incredible String Band played there', but can't because she's lost the keys.

And then there are the ghosts. Janet Joel mentions Elizabeth Owen, who searches the house for her lost jewellery; Gruffydd Evans, who can be heard playing his harp in the woods; wisps of smoke that become women; women who gawp at sleepers then disappear through walls.

And then there are the earthlights, the ha'ants, the will o' the wisps, whatever you want to call them. Local groundsmen and shepherds tell tales of mysterious lights above the hills, and the mansion itself, and in the gardens, too. No less a personage than Caradoc Evans, when living at New Cross, wrote in his journal:

> At 11:50 p.m. last Sunday I saw a light in the direction of Devil's Bridge[22]. I looked at it through a small telescope. It was a white globe and was rising higher and higher into the air... a smaller light appeared beneath it. This also rose in the air.... Both disappeared before 2:30 a.m. I reported the matter to the police[23].

And then there are the poets. Fiona Sampson, esteemed editor of *Poetry Review* and fine writer herself, once lived at Nanteos, in the stable flat. I meet her in the Wetherspoon's pub in the train station on one of her frequent visits back to Aberystwyth and she tells me about her time at Nanteos, the noises she'd hear from the derelict outbuildings at night, the owl which would perch on her windowsill and screech. As a child, she was taken to see the Holy Grail when it was sojourning in Hereford, but she can recall little about it. She does remember, though, the American poet Michael Donaghy choking in the Indian restaurant that used to be on the pier; he swallowed a piece of that bark that's used to flavour pilau rice and had to make himself sick in the toilet. Part of Fiona's childhood is in Aberystwyth; she grew up next to Paul Henry on the Waun (always such connections, concatenations, in Aberystwyth), whose mother, she tells me, was the town soprano who didn't get on with Fiona's own mother, who was a violin teacher (Fiona herself is a classically trained violinist. As is Matt Jarvis. See?). Both vied for the position of alpha female musician, it seems. Fiona went to a primary school up Primrose Hill which isn't there any more; in 1970 it slid down the cwm in a mudslide, after which she had to attend school in Chancery. She left the area aged twelve but returned in her late twenties to live in Llanafan and Nanteos. She set up the Aberystwyth Poetry Festival. Her wonderful poem 'Sestina for an Ice Age'[24] refers to this relocation. She tells me about the Nanteos lights, how they'd skim the grass, how they appeared to be solid objects, how they'd terrify the gardeners. 'I like to lie in the wood's cover/like a Welshman', she writes in 'Green Thought'[25]. She did a lot of that in the woods that outlie the odd mansion.

And Dafydd Prys spent much of his youth (he's still young) in Nanteos, both the mansion itself and the gatehouse (where his parents still live). I meet him in the Ship and Castle pub on a Thursday night, one of the oldest pubs in town. Terrific old painting on the back wall, of a ship, and, ahem, a castle. Beer festivals are held here with great frequency. Tonight, Jilted John is on the jukebox. Still makes me laugh. Dafydd worked on *Planet* with John Barnie but is now setting up his own publication, *Blue Tattoo*[26]. He tells me that Mary Anne Constantine – daughter of the well-known poet David – may fill John's shoes. Dafydd, too, saw the Holy Grail as a kid. He tells me things about Nanteos that the guidebooks don't; that, despite it being the same building that was completed in 1710, there is no damp inside the house, and that the Powell who was killed in World War One was shot after the armistice, and in the back, probably by his own men. The current owner of Nanteos also owns Alexandra Hall, on the promenade, which is now student accommodation, but was lying derelict for over a decade; he's a property developer, buying up old places, selling off the antique furniture, making a fortune. Dafydd stayed overnight in the mansion recently as a guardian, alone, and saw and felt 'absolutely nothing supernatural'. Growing up there, he 'wished every day' that he would see or otherwise experience something out of the usual, but he never did. The old story about Nanteos, he says, is that people with no connections to the area at all buy it up and do nothing with it. Even some of the land is now being sold off.

(An aside about *Blue Tattoo*, while Dafydd's here; he was going to continue *Cambrensis* – the Wales-based short story magazine – after the death of founder and editor Arthur Smith, but he sees Smith as irreplaceable. *Blue Tattoo* will, hopefully, fill the gap that the passing of *Cambrensis* has left. 'Nothing groundbreaking,' he says, 'but something that will make people stop for one second and go ooo'. Which is a grand aim. For the first issue, he's setting one of my own short stories to graphic images. I'm excited about it. Ooo.)

'Anarchy in the UK' comes on the jukebox. It's a song I still love and revere. We talk about punk and Dafydd says: 'It was more than people just reacting, it gave them hope.' His brother, Owain, enters the pub. Contrasting with Dafydd, he found Nanteos scary: 'The trees scared me. The atmosphere is built for fear. Inside the house, you were safe. Outside, you weren't.' I ask if Owain might be the sibling more sensitive to contact from a world behind this one. 'Maybe,' he says, 'which is why Daf wanted to see things.' Dafydd responds: 'I am a walking advert for why ghosts don't exist. I'm disappointed, to be honest.'

My friends Ossian and Eleanor enter the pub. The night just slides away.

*

Recent promotional bumf has presented the mansion as a place for weddings and 'stag nights, private dinners, business conferences, for arts and educational organisations [to hold] meetings and presentations of all kinds.... Overnight accommodation is limited, but transport can be laid on to and from the town centre'. But it seems that business enterprises fail, when foisted on Nanteos. The house doesn't seem to welcome such things. The odd magic that clings to and is emitted by the place appears fiercely oppositional to any sort of profiteering, even of a humble and low-key stripe. Maybe the phantoms would sooner see it crumble than be made magnetic to the paying punter. Poets sip from Christ's cup in wraith-light, attended by ghosts. In English, 'Nanteos' translates as 'stream of the nightingale'. That says a lot.

THE BUARTH AND PLASCRUG

Plascrug is the pedestrian umbilicus that links, by foot or bicycle, Aberystwyth with Llanbadarn. It's about two miles long, beginning at

Yr Ysgol Cymraeg primary school and ending next to the bus gyratory and the cluster of large stores behind it on the Rheidol Retail Park – B-Wise, Iceland, Lidl, etc. Cheap goods of all kinds. There's the rugby club down here, and it's looked over by the tax office windows, and a field behind hedges and trees about half-way down used, some years ago, to host fetes and parties and fairs; they were popular, but happened only a few times, I don't know why. There's a children's playground too which used to house monstrous metal sculptures of giant spiders for children to climb on; horrific things to see on your way back from one of the aforementioned shindigs, when you'd ingested nothing that a celeb-chef (or, indeed, a doctor) would recommend. The sculptures have changed, now; they're worth a photograph but today they're being clambered on by hordes of children in their playful panic and pointing a camera, these days, in the general direction of children who aren't one's own is enough to land you on a certain register for a decade or so, so I don't bother. There's a slimy, chickweed-choked ditch on the right of Plascrug, which runs alongside the cricket pitches for the entire length. It's a horrible, mucussy little rivulet that, surprisingly, teems with life; I remember once, other plans being thwarted, sitting on the edge of that ditch to sulk and slowly realizing that there was an aquatic zoo in there. Red-bellied sticklebacks nosed wearily out of their nests; water-boatmen cast cheerleader shadows on the mud bed, the tiny ripples of water at their feet like pom-poms. A vole peered out of its burrow on the opposite bank, saw me, and ducked back in again. Or it might've been a rat. Probably was, really. Ram's horn snails. Caddis fly larvae. A fascinating, icky little ditch.

Plascrug is separated from Ffordd Llanbadarn by a huge cemetery. The dead loom large and cautionary in Aberystwyth, as they do in most Welsh towns. Set into the graveyard walls are recesses that contain benches; we'll see this feature again, at the castle. The benches aren't quite long enough for a homeless person to stretch out on, but they look quite snug nonetheless, sheltered from the rain. The

graveyard once had a strange frequenter; late at night, a wheelchair-bound man would move between the stones, surrounded by a score or so of small dogs, running and jumping and frantic but always in complete silence, man and hound. An eerie thing to witness but probably not as spooky or mysterious as our earnest conversations around sputtering gas fires in pubs would make it out to be. Just a feller of restricted mobility walking his dogs in peace, that's all. But the silence. That really was a wee bit unnerving.

Railway track on left. Tax offices on right, dull and foursquare and functional – I've seen buildings like this, many times over, in eastern bloc countries. Just looking at them makes me feel tired and threatened and like giving in (although the people within, here, are pleasant and helpful. Almost takes some of the sting out of being forced to pay for an illegal war and occupation). Opposite is a bare patch of concrete where a public lavatory once stood; it was a renowned cottage, now obliterated with shame-exorcising ruthlessness. The bared wall bears graffiti; a few Banksy-style 'ELVIS's (again) and 'THIS TOWN IS FULL OF SHEEP'. Behind that wall is the Rheidol Retail Park, aforementioned. It's perhaps best not to stand too close to the B-Wise walls on a windy day; I mixed the cement that went into their construction. Built by two brickies from Milford Haven who would, with predictable regularity, ask me to go and fetch a loaf so they could mop up the mortar I'd sloppily supplied them with. Dead funny.

Here, at the new roundabout which often backs traffic up to the top of Penglais Hill, facing Stormriders, turn right and continue up to the close-packed red-brick terraces of the Buarth. Timber and coal were once stored in the vicinity, as the name suggests ('buarth' or 'yard'), and still were, in fact, when I first moved to the town; the space between the train station and Plascrug was, then, a huge coalyard behind a row of derelict shops. The Buarth streets look more Valleys or industrial northern England than mid-Wales, and at the top of their slopes, in a prefab-type building, stood the Mercator

Centre, home of the Welsh Literature Abroad offices (and workplace of some of the loveliest, sweetest people I've ever done business with). They're part of the European network of literature centres ('...making literature travel'), and I pick some *Transcript* brochures up from there[27], the 'European internet review of books and writing', which pushes itself as 'a unique window on the diversity and vitality of contemporary European writing, with texts, reviews, interviews, features and special issues on lesser known literatures.... *Transcript* will take you on exciting journeys of the mind'. They're not exaggerating. The Literature Across Frontiers scheme is a grand one, promoting as it does, through seminars and festivals and conferences, literatures 'written in the less widely used, minority and regional languages of Europe', including Catalan, Basque, Irish, Welsh, Flemish, Shetlandic, Scots and Scots Gaelic. I wouldn't go so far as to say that this enterprise could only be based in a town that has expansive identity politics as expressed through language at it's heart, but I'm glad that it does. Here, as elsewhere in Aber, a kind of cultural and political defiance is writ large; not just an insistence on an identity threatened by creeping homogeneity, but an expression of that identity through communication, on equal terms, with others who feel that threat and work against it. Eluned Morgan's booklet 'Minority Languages in the European Union' is stacked up in the Mercator offices; it's of necessity a fairly dry document, discussing as it does the need for further economic support for minority languages in various parliamentary and jurisprudential fora, but it contains fascinating potted histories of minority tongues throughout Europe, as well as statistics on their recovery or decline. It's also written with a committed heart unafraid of emotional expression that is largely absent from publications of this sort. I also picked up the latest issue of the *Mercator Media Forum*, an annual journal 'to promote discussion and the flow of information between those who work in the non-state languages of the European union'. Lead essay in this issue is by Panayote Dimitras, 'Minorities and Media in Greece', and, in his editorial, George Jones writes that Greece 'is unmatched in the EU for hostility towards its linguistic minorities and even denial of their existence', which fact surprised me. The journal underlines the cruciality of the web and projects like Mercator to the continuing survival of minority languages (and, consequently, peoples) not just in the EU but globally.

Ned Thomas, who lives just off the Buarth in an 1870s-built townhouse in an old part of the town below the hospital, explains the term 'Mercator' to me. Old maps and atlases, he says, had projections wherein the south of the world appeared smaller than the north, because the dominant languages tended to have their country of origin in the north. So Gerardus Mercator, Flemish geographer and cartographer, made a kind of linguistic map of the world, a consciously politically-charged act[28]. The Mercator Media Project grew into Welsh Literature Abroad and Literature Across Frontiers, and one of its current projects, with which Ned is heavily involved, is the development of a bi-lingual (Welsh and English) version of the Open Office software. Objective One funding has been secured. This is under the Mercator umbrella, as are various other theatre, film and TV projects, as well as literary ones.

It's a beautiful spring day when I go to see Ned, and I'm bleary from the bowlful of vegetable curry I ate for lunch at the Carvery. Like John Barnie and Robat Gruffydd, if you know anything about Aberystwyth, or indeed recent Welsh political history in general, then you'll probably know something about Ned Thomas. He's the man who wrote *The Welsh Extremist*. He's the man who started *Planet*. He's the man who used to run the University of Wales Press, whose biggest achievement, he will tell me, was the first Welsh/English dictionary; 'such a needed book'. He's the man who puts aside the breezeblock-sized biography of Gwynfor Evans he's reading when I appear in the grand living-room of his stately townhouse and sits me down with a cup of tea and a plate of chocolate biscuits. Pud.

To many, Ned Thomas *is* modern Wales; one wouldn't exist without the other. He towers within contemporary Wales's cultural pantheon. He has a fascinating personal history; he travelled through-out Britain shortly after World War Two, following his father's work, which was to do with the re-construction of Blitz-hit cities. His was a Welsh-speaking household, but based in England; often, however, he'd go to Bangor, to stay with his grandparents. After the war, Ned's dad was sent to Germany to assist in the 'de-Nazification' process; the family lived on the banks of the Ruhr, next to a bombed waste-land: 'mile upon mile of devastation', says Ned. He remembers American aircraft spraying the bombsite with DDT to counteract the infection from the rotting bodies buried there.

On return from Germany, the Thomases moved to Pennal, by Aberdyfi[29]. Ned schooled in Machynlleth, moved to Sheffield, went to university in Oxford, in the year below Dennis Potter. National Service obligations claimed a couple of years of his life, after which he moved to London as a journalist, then to Salamanca in Spain, where, in the sixteenth century, Frey Luis de Leon was seized by the Inquisition and imprisoned for years; on his release, he returned to the lecture hall in which he'd been arrested and continued precisely from where he was forced to leave off with the words 'as I was saying yesterday'. Ned used this quote to re-start *Planet* in 1985 after it had lain dormant since 1979, in disillusionment at the referendum result of that year (in which Wales basically voted 'no' to devolution from Westminster).

Ned worked on *The Times* in London, then went to Russia in the late 60s, leaving just before the invasion of Prague and returning to London where he edited the Russian-interest magazine *Anglia*, which sold in six figures to those Russians hungry for information about western culture (there was a lot of such people). Ned's job was to pinpoint what was unlikely to get past the Russian censors. The Foreign Office funded it, but because it was a quarterly, there was ample time to pore over and dissect the articles. The last straw came when Ned commissioned an article from a *Spectator* journalist about UK taxation; in those days, unearned income tax was high, but in Russia, well-paid people didn't pay any income tax at all – in Ned's words, they had 'bottomless bank accounts'. Ned had two children by this time, so he moved back to Wales (he always spoke Welsh, but couldn't read or write it very well). He didn't have a job, but sold up in London anyway, and moved to Llangeitho, by Tregaron, and worked freelance. He wrote *The Welsh Extremist* in 1970, the genesis of which is explained clearly and succinctly in its introductory chapters.

Planet began in 1971, and initially ran until 1979, because Ned reasoned that if the referendum of that year was going to return a 'YES' vote, which it was expected to do, then Wales would need a publication like *Planet* more frequently, but a 'NO' vote would mean that *Planet*'s 'reformist line hadn't really worked', so something other would be required. Hence the setting up of *Arcade* in 1979 by Ned, John Osmond and Robin Reeves, a more 'downmarket and popular' publication. Sales were reasonable, but the Arts Council grant was withdrawn. The Queen visited Cardiff in the month that 80,000 steel workers lost their jobs; that issue of *Arcade* had a cover depicting the royal family with a speech-bubble reading 'let them eat cake'. And so end of funding.

The first version of *Planet* began shortly after the '69 investiture of Prince Charles as Prince of Wales, 'at a time of secret police and language activism'. William Crawshay of Merthyr supported the magazine which was considered a militant journal in the 70s and the shutting down of it, Ned says, was 'purely voluntary... I don't think institutions should last forever'. But it left a gap, so Ned appointed John Barnie to re-start it, partly because of his 'green' credentials, which were of a piece with *Planet*'s conservationist agenda[30]. So *Planet* Mk II came shortly after the Miner's Strike, at a time of rare unity in Wales (forged through a desire simply to not be Thatcherite).

I've read *The Welsh Extremist*, several times, and I've just exhorted you to do the same (if, of course, you haven't already), but I have to ask Ned: What prompted it? He replies that he saw a large gap between what was being said and thought in Wales and how that was being seen over the border: 'I wrote it for England, really'. It received a positive review from the great Raymond Williams and sold very well in Wales, but not so well in England. In the 70s, 'English-language Wales was quite sleepy', and, pre-Thatcher, not a lot, politically, was going on (although it was in Welsh-language Wales, of course). The book was 'an act of communication between Welsh-language culture and the world that read English', and letters from readers at the time revealed to Ned the depth of the emotional well he was tapping. 'Communication across barriers is the thing that has always driven me', he says; hence Mercator, LAF, etc., also *Planet* itself: ' I had a feeling that what got in between the Wales I knew and the wider world was a terrible provincialism that I associated with the *Western Mail* and George Thomas', who was House of Commons Speaker and Secretary of State and was caricatured in *Planet*'s first issue, which the *Guardian* reprinted.

That provincialism has, in my opinion, re-surfaced, in a new, pinched, isolationist and mean form. I understand how that can be born in a forcibly wizened and attenuated soul, but I don't under-stand its celebration. Thankfully, John and Ned and Robat have people like Dafydd Prys and Francesca Rhydderch as part of their progeny; otherwise, I'd see reason for despair. The English rugby fans sing 'should've built a wall, not a bridge', and at times I see people in Wales doing just that. But I also see others weakening the mortar (shades of B-Wise) and some light starts to shine through. Which metaphor I've already exhausted so I'll leave it there.

I ask Ned about Aberystwyth. He's lived here since 1979, largely for familial reasons; Penweddig school had opened and he wanted to send his children there, and not to the English-language school in Tregaron. The town is not, for Ned, Abercuawg[31], because it 'gets some of it's energy from friction' (Fran Rhydderch, editor of the *New*

Welsh Review, will say a similar thing, later), such as the often abrasive accommodation between the two languages. The setting up of Pantycelyn – a Welsh-speaking, mixed-sex hall of residence – provoked opprobrium: 'This will undermine morality!' Indeed, the Aber Labour party was run by people who were against Pantycelyn. So the Liberals took Labour's seat. The town is built on friction.

The original Aber townspeople, Ned says, were rural-born, and are now completely assimilated and now Gown is dominating Town: 'West Wales and the Valleys is an Objective 1 area, but look at it more closely; if Ceredigion is below the average income, then imagine what the income is like outside Aberystwyth'. The town is unbalanced; the ratio of professional people to students in relation to other sections of the populace is disproportionate. This isn't so noticeable in a larger town. Aber's institutions create a focus for people from other parts of Wales, so the town grows, giving rise to more friction, 'which isn't always destructive, it can be creative', says Ned, and I agree.

On my way out, he gives me a copy of 'The Pencarreg Three', a booklet of transcribed speeches made in Carmarthen Crown Court after the switching off of the Pencarreg transmitter (remember Robat?). It's an extremely important document for left liberal politics anywhere, although its focus, of course, is Welsh-speaking Wales, and the dishonouring of his promise to set up a Welsh-speaking TV channel by William Whitelaw. I'll quote Ned, from the booklet:

> It slowly dawned on me that a nation which would accept the treat-
> ment we had received over the fourth channel would accept anything
> that was done to it. For me our action at Pencarreg was a small
> gesture of non-acceptance.... As I write these words Dr. Gwynfor
> Evans has announced that he is willing to fast unto death, if neces-
> sary, over the matter of the Welsh television channel. That can only
> make us all redouble our efforts.

Ah, Gwynfor Evans – the man whose biography[32] Ned was reading when I first met him. The man who died in 2004 and whose cortege through Aberystwyth stretched for a solemn mile. The man who Hywel Williams, *Guardian* columnist, called '*y mab darogan*'[33] – 'the prophesied son', who had 'deeply felt intuitions about the interplay of religion, language and soil'. He's Aber-linked, too.

I leave Ned's house, blinking in the sunlight. The curry's been digested and I don't feel sluggish anymore. Where am I? Ah yes, the Buarth. I'd forgotten.

GLAN YR AFON INDUSTRIAL ESTATE

Glan yr Afon. The industrial estate. Same as any other industrial estate outside any town or city anywhere in the country. Wide thoroughfares to facilitate the passage of trucks, big warehouses, storage depots. That kind of thing. The tip here is extremely neat with skips for wood, laminated wood, vegetation, glass, car batteries, electrical goods, etc. Its custodian evidently takes pride in keeping it kempt, and he does a great job. It's just up the way from Pulsar, which has an office on the top floor of Cambrian Supplies, and is a computer repair outfit which has helped me out of many a virus'd spot. Hugh and Duncan. They've both patiently and on many occasions talked me out of a panic over the telephone when a black hole in cyberspace has threatened to suck work into it, and they've installed new anti-virus software when the old stuff itself became infected and ill. It sometimes scares me, that world inside this laptop; the Pulsar people are guides, sherpas, fighting off the worms and Trojan horses and other vile bugs. Hooray for 'em.

There used to be a cheese factory on this estate that offered hard and horrible but needed temporary work to those in need of funds. A few weeks' worth of twelve hour shifts would be a visit to curdled hell but you'd come out of it with enough money to tide you over a similar length of time or to pay whichever debtor had inadvertently sent you there. You'd come out smelling not of roses but vaguely of vomit, but you could send the wolves skulking back into the woods for a while. The factory's moved, now, to, I believe, just outside Lampeter. The café's still there, though, where in the early morning you could come

off shift and eat a great greasy breakfast before heading home to welcome slumber. Or you could go there and meet your mates coming off their shift and do the same thing. You'd have been up all night, partying; they'd have been placing blocks of sweaty processed cheese on a conveyor belt all night. You'd both have pale faces and red-rimmed eyes and you'd both be yawning and nodding into your full

English and you'd both be smelling slightly of sick but only one of you would be smiling.

The estate ends abruptly at the Cwm Rheidol side, to the east, furthest from Aberystwyth, and tiny lanes lead off into woods and fields and it begins to feel wild. Again, typical Aberystwyth; the urban and the rural adjacent. Sneeze and you'll miss when one becomes the other. It really is startlingly abrupt; the estate's clank and concrete and then instantly the buzz of bees, the shade of trees. Mud and hawks. Follow these lanes and they'll take you deep into the green beauty of the Rheidol valley where even the very concept of 'industrial estate' could be on another planet. But I'll go there some other time. I'm already bored of wandering around warehouses and there's only so much orange tea and so many egg rolls I can stand before bloatedness and boredom and flatulence set in.

Bus stop.

CLARACH/WALLOG

There are three ways up Constitution Hill, or 'Consti'; straight up, the quickest and steepest; up Cliff Terrace and around the back, which is three times as long, but affords great views; or on the funicular. This being late winter that's not running and time is at a premium so I go for the first option. And then spend half an hour panting into a cup of tea and an apple and sultana Go Ahead bar at the top of the hill before the first whiff of breath returns to my lungs. There's a tremendous view of the town from up here, but I can't appreciate it with my vision swimming in a crimson haze like this.

It's a wonderful walk, along the coastal path from Aberystwyth to Borth. High and exposed and with the briny wind off the sea far below sucking snot from your nose and tears from your eyes it's exhilarating, especially on a blowy day. As you descend into the holiday village of Clarach you pass through a pine woods where, often, Blair Witchy-style wooden sculptures dangle from the branches; pentagrams and stick men. Either kids messing around or something more sinister, they can be really quite eerie in the still and wind-whistling trees. They range from no bigger than your thumb to entire trees half-felled and pushed together to form a giant shape. They can be creepy, if you're in the right mood to feel that way, and today they seem to suit the emptiness of Clarach, 'quiet as the grave in the winter', to quote Liz Allan[34]. Deserted statics and boarded up chalets. Pubs, Spar, chippy, all closed. Drizzle and wind across the dodgems and slides. Fun fair waterlogged. Rain bubbling from the holes of the Crazy Golf. In a couple of months there'll be glitterballs and Elvis impersonators, spangly-jacketed MCs with lambchop sideburns and thinning quiffs, Brummie accents and oniony smells. Mechanical shrieking and blooping from the amusement arcades. Fisticuffs in the pubs and discos and used condoms on the cliff paths. Now, though – tumbleweeds, although the swimming pool and leisure centre and attached bar are open. I don't go in. Continue past it to resume the cliff top path. Pretty soon you'll be able to see Wallog, jutting like a lapping tongue into the steel-grey sea.

It's also called Sarn Gynfelyn, and is an impressive structure that reaches five miles or so into the sea although only the first few hundred feet are visible. 'Sarn' can be translated as 'causeway', which, as John Gilbey has pointed out[35], 'hints at a lore that speaks of ancient sunken lands'. It's not man-made – 'it is thought to be a morraine feature dating from the last Ice Age', Liz Allan reckons – but it can seem that way. You can walk on it, out into the sea. See the stones tumbling into the dark water on each side, turn around to face the shore and the fine stone house, the arched lime kiln on the littoral and the robust sea wall that 'spell out a prosperous past, when coastal craft grounded here to unload the limestone which, when processed, would help feed the bitter upland soil' (Gilbey again). It's a beautiful house, inhabited only intermittently by, I believe, teams of outward-bounders or geologists, something like that.

On summer days, I have swum with seals off Sarn Gynfelyn whilst potatoes boiled in a pan of seawater on the shore. I have shared

sandwiches with mangy dogs that flinched and cowered when I raised my arm to throw them food. Not quite Taliesin, I know, but....

There's an otherworldly feel to the place, sometimes, especially when you're on your own. Cormorants abound and roost in large numbers on the sea-cliffs and the air crackles wherever those liminal birds gather. Not even the scurf of garbage that marks the tideline nor the rotting clumps of seaweed and dead creatures and the foul smell they give off can weaken this sensation. Adds to it, in fact. It's peculiar. It calls to mind H.G. Wells, although I don't really know why that should be.

I could continue up out of Wallog and onto the path, but recent torrential rains have turned it quaggy and I've sunk ankle-deep several times already, getting here. The path that veers off at a right angle will, I know, be muddier, but will soon become tarmac. I take it. Honeysuckle and red campion. Squabbling robins. A dry road that will, after a few miles, take me down into Borth.

BORTH/YNYSLAS AND CANTRE'R GWAELOD

Strictly speaking, Borth should really be included in the 'Hinterlands' section, but the road from Wallog has neatly led me here and sometimes neatness is too hard to resist. It's a town in itself, not really a suburb of Aberystwyth, with its own schools and churches (of course) and pubs, but being primarily a holiday resort, much of it shuts down in the winter, when the town seems tugged towards the amenities in the much larger settlement six miles or so south.

The *Rough Guide* calls it 'drab', which it isn't, really, but it's certainly somewhat odd. The town consists basically of one long street running parallel to the sea behind ugly concrete defences with the great expanse of Cors Fachno, the bog, behind it, reaching flatly to the hazy humps of the Cambrian mountains. It's picturesque, after a fashion; a kind of Wild West stage-set feel pervades. It was once an important herring port, with trade to Derwenlas and Machynlleth along the Dyfi river, but the arrival of the railway line in Aberystwyth in 1864 put a stop to that[36]. In the summer months, it heaves; in the winter, it shudders bleakly in the gales off the Celtic Sea that batter the boarded up shops and houses and all it lacks is tumbleweeds.

It's the place where, in the early 1900s, William Hope Hodgson

wrote one of his most truly unhinged books. Hodgson was a bodybuilder who knew judo and who ran away to sea at the age of thirteen, 'a muscle-bound mystic... bloated with visions', to quote China Mieville[37]. *The House on the Borderland* tells the story of a man who lives in a big seaside mansion with his sister, Mary, and his dog, Pepper. The setting is supposedly Ireland, but it's recognisably Borth; there are references to 'a vast plain', 'an enormous amphitheatre of mountains', and an 'immense silent sea'. On a night-time foray into the mountains, the man sees monsters – a giant ass wearing a belt of human skulls; pig-things that 'lope' on their hind legs and peer in through windows. He finds a pit in the mountains into which he abseils, finds a 'great cellar' which floods and, presumably, drowns the 'swine-things'.

And then it gets weird. Back at his house, the days start to pass in seconds, literally – the sun and stars scoot across the sky, the hands of the clock move so fast that they whistle: 'The constant blur of the world-noise on my hearing'. The sun becomes a comet. The man, in a matter of hours, collapses into decrepitude, but continues to live until so much time has passed that the furniture in his room is just dust on the floor. He witnesses the heat-death of the sun into 'a vast dead disk'. He meets his lost love at the end of the world, who is taken from him again. Two 'Central Suns' appear, one with a face of 'tortured woe'. He drifts out into the mountains again, maybe only in dream this time, to address the 'lurking horrors that peopled those supreme heights'. He returns to his house to find the dust of his dog, and then there's something about a new dog, which is wounded in his kennel by a 'Terror', and the wound sprouts a white fungus. The dog licks the man's hand and the man then grows covered by 'a terrible mass of living corruption' and a vile, unnamed thing crawls up from his cellar.

And there it ends. It's berserk. It's deranged. It's hallucinogenically awful. I wonder at the point of it, although I fully comprehend how it came out of such a place as Borth. It's one of those books that stays in your mind, fizzing out puzzlement, for years. There's no blue plaque on the house in which Hodgson wrote it, but his name does appear on the war memorial on the cliff above the town. The First World War killed him, so I can't ask him his thoughts on this strange little town, but I can ask Lindsay Ashford, who's very much alive, resident writer with three novels published by Honno and a Quick Read, *The Rubber Woman*, published by Accent Press. She loves her  adopted town (she was born in Wolverhampton); the stories here about the *cors gwrach*, the 'witch of the bog', a seven-foot-tall hag who appears out of mist to pass on a hideous disease with her touch; the carnival, biggest in the county apparently, which involves such antics as a competition to stay upright the longest on the sea in a homemade contraption, which apparently echoes the feat of an ancient tribal chieftain rejecting a foreign claim to the land (yes, I'm confused, too). Lindsay loves the juxtaposition here of bog and sea, 'fantastic for curing writer's block', she says, and loves the mixed population of the village; the indigenous Welsh, the hippies, the incomers, those re-located there from the West Midlands because of problems to do with drink and drugs and domestic violence etc.. All these groups come together at carnival time. Unites the village. The summer crowds threaten to make it unbearable, but Lindsay then escapes to Ynyslas, which huge expanses of sand with views across the estuary to Aberdyfi ensure that she never feels 'hemmed in', even for a person who is, 'by nature, claustrophobic'. She tells me that 'the sea is always different. . . I'm much more at ease next to it'.

She's not wrong. At the war memorial, high above the town on Rhiw Fawr, the sense of space is exhilarating, immense. Land and water are continually at battle here; the reclaimed land of the bog to the right is a vast flat field of brown and green, traceried by the silver ribbons of streams and rivulets and temporary home to many migrant waders and waterfowl – wigeon, mallard, teal, pintail, and 'the only flock of Greenland white-fronted geese regularly occurring in Wales' (Liz Allan again). The sea, at low tide today, appears a deep blue from up here, all the way to Ireland. The solid and the liquid are always at each other's throats, here. Unusual things happen to the mind in places like this; the soul as the centre of an elemental tug-of-war. Succumbing either way carries the suggestion of reduction; that solidity, say, will offer only one experience. Yet accepting the flux means settling for unsurety. What to do? Maybe that's why Hodgson could unleash his demons here. Maybe this is the area where he found them in the first place. Or they found him.

Descend the hill, into the town proper. The circular tower of the Nisa shop replaced the old and ramshackle Spar, after that burnt, or was burnt, down. There are rumours that a restaurant is to be built on its upper floors, but not for another year or so. That'd be good; fresh fish with a view of the dazzling sea. After a much-needed all-day brekkie and mug of orange tea at the Limit caff with my face burning from the exposed walk's flaying by the wind, I explore the one long street that, really, is Borth. Not that there's a great deal to explore, but I while away an interesting hour or so in the warren of cluttered rooms above the Friendship Inn ('FROCK OFF!' says a sign outside, but in a friendly way). It's a great pub, the Friendship, delightfully named, with compact novels written on the toilet walls. It's been an inn since 1860, when Captain David Hughes obtained a spirit license and named the hostelry after his ship. The antique shop upstairs is crammed with interesting junk; books, postcards, costumery, faded photographs of people becoming sepia spectres, china, glassware, jewellery, furniture, brass, copper, silver.... The smell is musty and lovely. A thousand lives hinted at in these stacked-up treasures.

White-painted footprints of a dinosaur or thunderbird pace the pavement outside. A prank leftover from the carnival, maybe. A sign

points towards the Animalarium but I don't go. I've been before, and it made me sad; animals in cages, offensive to both the outer and inner eye, and because the menagerie's space is restricted, well... the leopard's coat latticed with the impress of mesh. True, like all zoos, this one is part of a breeding programme for various animals whose habitat and/or very existence is under threat, and that's laudable, but personally I'd rather not see them claw at glass or steel or repetitively tread grooves in the grass or concrete of their enclosures. Some moments of my visit I remember fondly; the meerkats; the kookaburra trying to offer his mate, who was having none of it and kept haughtily turning her head away, the present of a dead mouse; the friendly raccoon. Wonderful creatures, all (and the snakes and crocs and jungle cats). I remember how a group of tiny marmosets went shriekingly hysterical before my face, screaming, leaping, slapping the glass, until the removal of my sunglasses, in an instant, calmed them. See? No big, hungry, predator-eyes here. But the faces on people who gaze at imprisoned animals... I've seen similar expressions in strip-clubs. Not for me.

So I go down onto the pebble beach instead to watch the waves and wait for my train. Anterior to the ebbing waves I can see the shapes of the petrified forest that may have given rise to the story of *Cantre'r Gwaelod*, the drowned land[38]. Once, the story goes, part of Cardigan Bay was a very fertile low-lying land surrounded by dykes and floodgates. On the night of a thanksgiving festival, which happened to be stormy, the guardian of the gates, Seithenyn, got drunk and fell asleep and forgot to close the gates and the wind drove the sea through to drown the land and all that lived on it. One of the area's main walls is said to be the causeway at Wallog, where we've already been. On still nights you can hear the church bells tolling beneath the waves, et cetera. Over a thousand people were drowned.

Strange how, in Wales, mythology often has a real-world counter-part. *Cantre'r Gwaelod* is echoed in the story of Tryweryn. Dream and reality blur, but don't let that blind you to what your eyes see and ears hear; suffering is very real. Terry Davies's book *Borth: A Seaborn Village*, is an indispen-sable reference work to the area. He explains the etymol-ogy of the strange word 'Wallog', how it may stem from old Welsh meaning 'unusual, quirky, or not quite right', and how 'the phenomenon of the causeway promoted Other-world possibilities' (or simply that it might come from the name 'Gwallawg', the 'hairy

one'. I prefer the former). Of the *Cantre'r Gwaelod* tale, he writes that it was the survivors of that flooding 'who discovered [the poet] Taliesin as a foundling and gave him his name'. Thomas Love Peacock re-worked the story in his novel *The Misfortunes of Elphin* in 1829.

My mind draws leylines between *Cantre'r Gwaelod* – Tryweryn – New Orleans as I wait for the train at the empty station. Deaths by drowning, not only of the physical. Rising waters, incompetence and greed. I have a half hour wait, at least. The destructive power of water in alliance with the selfish idiocies of men is terrifying. Don't indulge a pissed-off Poseidon. To kill time, I cross the railway lines and tickle a couple of donkeys between their ears. Mist comes in over the bog, making statues of the grazing horses and veiling in gauze the great black church that dominates the flatlands about. Had I the time and energy, I could join the Mal Evans Way at the YHA hostel towards Ynyslas sands and walk the eighteen miles to Devil's Bridge. Maybe another day. Train's twenty minutes late.

DEVIL'S BRIDGE

The A4120, the twisting road that takes you from Penparcau to Devil's Bridge, runs through deep chapel Wales. The names of the hamlets bow to the historical dominance of the capel; there's Moriah, the name of the hill upon which Isaac was sacrificed[39], and also Pisgah, which has strong Mosaic connections, not least because it was from a place of that name that he first beheld the promised land[40].

The scenery is striking, and the plains at valley bottom fertile, but no more so than many other places in Wales; but enticing misnomers are global[41]. The landscape is best seen from the window of the Henffordd Arms, literally 'Old Road', but it's called the Halfway Inn in English because it's supposedly exactly half way between Aberystwyth and Devil's Bridge. It has a genuine set of stocks outside the door bearing the legend 'I DOTH REPENT'. The neck and wrist-holes are very small. Must've pinched. Chafed a fair bit, too. The pub does good food and cracking cider. Moses, I'm sure, would've blanched.

Devil's Bridge itself is the terminus for the Vale of Rheidol steam train that leaves from Aberystwyth, and which once would've taken slate miners to the workings at Aberffrwd and Cwm Rheidol and other places along that lovely valley. It caters to the tourist trade nowadays, of course – those wanting to see the three stacked bridges and the waterfalls and the Punchbowl, a huge and smooth foaming cauldron formed by the thundering waters. The nomenclature is interesting; the English title highlights the Devil's rôle in the tale, whilst the Welsh – Pontarfynach – highlights the monk's. Three roads (A4120, B4343, and the B4574) converge on the three bridges over the churning river Mynach, one on top of the other; the road bridge on the top, dating from 1901, the stone bridge below that from 1753, and, below that, the original monk's bridge, dating from the eleventh century and reputedly built by the monks from Strata Florida abbey. You can lean over the parapet to see the bridges but it really is worth paying the entrance fee to go through the turnstiles and stand beneath them. They're impressive, as is the Mynach Falls walk; the scenery is magnificent, but not for the vertiginously-afflicted, especially the nearly-sheer Devil's Staircase. George Borrow loved this place; he describes it, in *Wild Wales*, as being 'thronged with tourists even then'. He points out the cave 'occupied in old times by the Wicked Children, the mysterious Plant de Bat, two brothers and a sister, robbers and murderers', which is intriguing, but I can't find any reference to the legend elsewhere. And of the Bridge itself, he calls it 'a work which though crumbling and darkly grey does much honour to the hand which built it, whether it was the hand of Satan or a monkish architect, for the arch is chaste and beautiful.... Gaze on these objects, namely, the horrid seething pot or cauldron, the gloomy volcanic slit, and the spectral, shadowy Devil's Bridge for about three minutes, allowing a minute to each, then scramble up the bank and repair to your inn[,] for you have seen enough'.

Ah, the sublime! Such sensitive souls.

So, yes, the naming of the bridge; either monk or devil. The story goes that an old lady, or, in some versions a monk, needing to cross the chasm, elicited the help of Satan in return for the soul of the first living thing to cross the bridge he would build overnight. She slept, and in the morning there was the bridge. She threw a stick across it, which was chased by her little dog. The Devil roared and stamped his foot and both he and dog disappeared in a huffy sulphorous puff. Poor damned dog.

And that's it. I don't think, really, that much can be read into it, concerning the piety of the Welsh or the dastardliness of the English[42]; rather, there's pragmatism in the Welsh name – the fact that the bridge was built by monks was passed down as simple unalterable fact, nothing more. It can perhaps be seen as symptomatic of the English need to turn Wales into the 'Most Sublimely Terrible', which of course has a socio-political redolence that needs exploring, but I and many others have done that, and will no doubt do so again. Today, standing on the bridge, all I'm reminded of is the magic moment in Michael Carson's moving and funny novel *Stripping Penguins Bare* when the protagonist Benson and his first real lover, Dr. Leptos, stand in the same spot looking down at the crashing waters and Leptos tells Benson the story behind the name (the old woman variant), with the twist that the old lady's cow had wandered across the river further down the valley and was now removed from her by the crevasse. When he's finished, Benson just nods and stares 'down at the pluming water. Me and Mum could have come up with a better one than that between tea and Criss Cross Quiz, he thought'. And then Leptos takes him back to his cottage where he subjects him to a graphic buggering, which manages to be both hilarious and sweet at the same time.

He's written brilliantly about Aberystwyth and it's environs, Michael Carson. He studied at the university in the 1970s. We'll meet him at length later, but for now, though, while you're here, you could do worse than take a stroll up to the Hafod estate, a 'Picturesque'-style retreat designed by Thomas Johnes and which hosted and entertained no less a poetic personage than William Blake. Peter Ackroyd[43] recounts how the great poet was commissioned to design and engrave a map as a guide to the estate, and how he may have been introduced to Johnes as a possible patron. The Bwa, or large free-standing sandstone arch at the estate's entrance, was designed to announce to night-time arrivals that they'd reached their destination; recently it was hit by a lorry, and cordoned off for repairs. Horseshit to exhaust, so the world spins. The Hafod mansion has long gone and the forest is now a working one; beautifully peaceful spots can be found along the banks of the trout river at the feet of the steep and thickly wooded slopes. The feeling is Alpine, maybe Canadian, definitely Welsh. I'd recommend that you do the Gentleman's Walk in a top hat and swinging a stout and silver-tipped cane.

Mike Parker, in his *Neighbours from Hell,* expounds on the 'Picturesque' ideal, and how it reached its zenith in the creation of the Hafod estate, and how it grew out of artistic theory to become 'an entire lifestyle, available for those wealthy and indulgent enough to pursue it'. It has at its heart a kind of Enlightenment superiority, a sense that untamed nature falls short and must be 'tweaked, fiddled with and framed, in order to satisfy its fussy devotees'. Undoubtedly, the Hafod estate bears the stamp of a fastidious hand, with its fripperies of follies and re-coursed rivers and gimcrack cataracts; but I like the ways in which wildness obtrudes, and it always does – bridges collapse, moles and ants undermine, vegetation spreads riotously, rapids shatter banks. Underneath those ordered hedgerows lie the bared bones of a million little victims. We can lament and deplore the psychological need to contain and control, but we can rejoice in its inevitable practical failure. The Hafod mansion itself crumbled and fell in 1959. See?

I stop at a bench by the rushing river to eat a sandwich. Two buzzards circle and mewl high above the pine-tops and I can see the muscular shadows of trout in the deep water under the overhanging bank on the far side of the river. I flip through the guides to the estate and walks that I picked up earlier at the information point in the car park and in the general stores in Devil's Bridge. I smudge them with salad cream from the sarnie and some smears of blood from bramble rips. It's March 21st, spring equinox, ostara or Alban Eiler. Beltaine – the 'brilliant fire'. The banishing of winter. Time of impending joy.

PONTRHYDFENDIGAID/YSTRAD FFLUR/ STRATA FLORIDA

Is this still Aberystwyth? Not really, no. It's more Tregaron or Rhayader. But it's within a short drive of the town and has inextricable links with the development of Llanbadarn and thus Aberystwyth itself so I'm going to include it briefly here. And anyway, I like the place very, very much.

The village itself doesn't offer much to detain or divert you, unless you're there in May when the annual eisteddfod takes place in the huge pavilion, able to seat 3,000 spectators. The Black Lion pub is a cracker; I heard a story recently – probably apocryphal – that a local woman with Lithuanian roots persuaded the landlord to host a *noson llawen* themed on her home country, with Lithuanian food, music,

talk etc. Over 200 people turned up. From remote mid-Wales to the last village on the Teifi, over 200 people of Lithuanian descent appeared out of hill-farms and hamlets to celebrate their heritage. Remarkable. Probably apocryphal, as I say, but you're guaranteed to be served by an eastern European at the bar. A Latvian, last time I went, and an Estonian before that; I told him about the night I spent drinking in the Valleys bar in Tallinn. He knew the place well, and told me that its name had ignited in him an interest in Wales which led to him pulling pints in a pub on the banks of the Teifi. Truly remarkable.

The name, Pontrhydfendi-gaid, translates into English as 'Bridge near the Ford of the Blessed Virgin', so the place is drenched in Christian lore and awe even without the ruins of the abbey at Strata Florida, or Ystrad Fflur, 'the valley of the flowers'. I love the abbey ruins, and the abutting graveyard, in which Dafydd ap Gwilym is buried beneath a huge and reaching yew-tree and wherein lies the grave of a single leg, 'the left leg and part of the thigh' (to quote the headstone) of Henry Hughes, cooper, interred in 1560. The rest of Henry and his friends and family had a wonderful and riotous wake for his lost limb, apparently.

A tremendous peace can be found here. There's not much physically remaining of the building itself, but what still stands evokes something mighty. It was Cistercian, founded in 1164 by Lord Rhys of Deheubarth, and grew quickly into an important agricultural and political and, of course, ecumenical centre. In 1238, Llywelyn the Great, aware of his impending demise, and fearful that his dream of a unified Wales would die with him, summoned the Welsh princes here to pledge allegiance to his son, Dafydd. Giraldus Cambrensis visited even before this, when beavers could be seen in the Teifi. He writes little about the place's appearance and situation, focusing instead, as was his wont, on the Cistercian monks from there who accompanied him on his journey (John of Whitland and Seisyll of Ystrad Fflur, if you're interested). George Borrow, as always, says more[44]; in Pontrhydfendigaid village, he finds 'much mire in the street, [and] immense swine lay in the mire, who turned up their snouts at me as I passed'. He wanders around the abbey ruins 'in which kings, saints and mitred abbotts were buried, and in which... was buried Dafydd ap Gwilym, the greatest genius of the Cimbric race and one of the first poets of the world'. He kisses Dafydd's yew tree and recites a bastardised version of Gruffydd Gryg's eulogy to the poet and then talks land-rent

and soil fertility with a local farmer who ask why the abbey was 'pulled down'. George replies: 'Because it was a house of idolatry to which people used to... worship images. Had you lived at that time you would have seen people down on their knees before stocks and stones, worshipping them, kissing them.... Horrible times, in which there were monks and friars and graven images'. Good ol' George. He's also on the lookout for the Llostlydan[45], 'a beast with a broad tail.... Clever beast he was; made himself house of wood in the middle of the river'. Giraldus could've helped him out, there.

CADW owns the site, now – the Welsh organisation for the preservation of historic buildings. I pick up a leaflet that tells me about the 'Strata Florida Open Day'. This underlines – as well it might – the vitality of the place to Welsh cultural identity, and outlines the current excavations and explorations, including one taking place in the nearby Abbey Wood, revealing the kiln where the famous, and striking, decorative clay floor tiles in the monk's cells were probably fired, as well as an ancient roadway. Coming attractions (or were coming, in the summer of 2006), include a demonstration of some ancient mining technologies and an exhibition of sculpture and utensils by a group of Irish sculptors called Umha Aois ('Bronze Age'). Life goes on, eh?

It's a hot day, so I buy a copy of Robinson and Platt's *Strata Florida Abbey/Talley Abbey* and take it to the shade of an arm of Dafydd's yew. Bees buzz and birds chirrup and a distant tractor grumbles in a field and the surrounding dead say nothing. Even Dafydd keeps his mouth shut. I'm happy. I like it here. I read about monasticism in twelfth century Wales and about the Cistercian resistance to colonialist organisation of the church, as well as to tenant servility. About the monks' habitual drunkenness. About how some of the floor tiles in the abbey appear to show a figure of a man in doublet and hood gazing into a mirror, which might represent pride or vanity. Strata Florida was suppressed in 1539, after which the buildings would've been partially dismantled, beginning with the lead roofs being melted down into ingots. According to Robinson and Platt, 'a record of 1555 tells of some ten tons from the abbey in storage at Aberystwyth'. So maybe the burying of Hughes's left pin wasn't the innocent japery it seems; maybe there was deliberate disrespect in that act.

I remember reading somewhere – I think it was in Fortean Times, but I haven't been able to track down the precise reference – that, in the woods above the abbey there is a spring, a holy well. It's remote, and practically inaccessible to anyone but an experienced rock climber, yet fresh flowers are regularly left at it. Who by and why is, of course, a mystery.

Well, everything crumbles. Time for the bus back to town.

Notes

1. 'No incomers'. Or something of that flavour.
2. In his *A Fashionable Watering Place*.
3. Remember the polar bear in sunglasses with the slogan 'it's frothy, man'? (Or was that Cresta?). I took part in a Corona taste-test once, about 6 years old. Like a dream come true.
4. In the collection *Ghost Country*.
5. Entering a property in the hours of daylight is 'breaking and entering'; after dark the same act is 'burglary'. One of the finer points of law, which seems pretty pernickety, really. But it can mean the difference of an extra year or two inside for the miscreant.
6. Penweddig – first Welsh-language school in Wales.
7. In *The Slipped Leash*.
8. Ditto.
9. See his entry in *Farmer*.
10. 'The Girls of Llanbadarn' in *Selected Poems*.
11. See the anonymous *Llanbadarn Fawr Through the Centuries*.
12. Iconotropy – the transformation of the symbols of an old religion into the symbols of a usurping orthodoxy, as evidenced in the horned and goat-footed Pan becoming the Christian Satan. Examined by Robert Graves in his *The White Goddess*.
13. In the editorial of 23rd March 2006.
14. Ditto.
15. Remember him? My, what a model of efficiency and achievement he turned out to be, eh?
16. On a more positive note, in 2006 Cyswllt Ceredigion Contact were named UK Drug Team of the year and awarded £10,000 at a ceremony in London (see Dylan Davies). So that's something.
17. Otherwise known as 'the Welsh Women's Press'.
18. And where the photographer Keith Morris had a studio. You'll meet Keith later.

19. It's a very steep hill, this. Once, I saw a truck snap its trailer bar on it, due to the severity of the gradient; the noise. Orange sparks like a geyser. No one was hurt.
20. See Janet Joel, *Nanteos*.
21. See his *The Bank Manager and the Holy Grail*.
22. Which, from New Cross, would've been in the direction of Dyffryn Paith, in which Nanteos is built.
23. See *Morgan Bible*.
24. In *Folding the Real*.
25. Ditto.
26. Available from PO Box 221, Aberystwyth, SY23 2XZ. Well worth checking out.
27. See the website transcript-review.org.
28. If I remember rightly, Y Cŵps pub had one of these maps pasted up on a wall, before the renovation.
29. And in which, recently, Glyndŵr's bones were found. Well, maybe Glyndŵr's. Or maybe just some other feller's who died in that area at the same time.
30. 'What distinguishes the protests in Wales from those in some parts of England to preserve the environment [is] that they converge on a special kind of consciousness which is a national consciousness', wrote Ned in *The Welsh Extremist*: 'All the threats are threats to the Welsh tradition, the protest is protest in the name of a shared past'.
31. 'Abercuawg' was the name R.S. Thomas gave to his quintessential Welsh village, his ur-tref, 'a town or village where the cuckoos sing'. See his *Selected Prose*.
32. *Gwynfor: Rhag Pob Brad* is written by Rhys Evans and published by Y Lolfa.
33. In 'The Great Redeemer'; see 'Works Consulted'.
34. See her *Walking the Cardigan Bay Coast* in 'Works Consulted'.
35. In his *Guardian* column 'Country Diary: Aberystwyth'. See 'Works Consulted'.
36. See J. Geraint Jenkins, *Ceredigion*.
37. In his introduction to Gollancz's latest omnibus of Hodgson's selected works. See 'Works Consulted'.
38. The name translates into something like 'lowland with a hundred towns', or it could refer to the old administrative division of land called 'a hundred'.
39. 'Take now thy son, thine only son Isaac, whom thou lovest, and get thee to the land of Moriah; and offer him there for a burnt offering upon one of the mountains': Genesis 2:22.
40. 'And Moses went up from the plains of Moab. . . to the top of Pisgah, that is over against Jericho, and the Lord showed him all the land of Gilead': Deuteronomy, 34:1.
41. 'Greenland', for instance, was so called because Erik the Red, who had been banished there, wanted to attract company from the northern frozen wastes, so he invented a name that would evoke fertility. See Fleisher in 'Works Consulted'.
42. And anyway, it should really be named after the little dog – Pont-ar-ci, perhaps. He's the loser in the whole business, after all. He got nothing out of it but an eternity of torment.
43. In his biography *Blake*. See 'Works Consulted'.
44. In, as always, *Wild Wales*.
45. Literally 'wide tail', but 'llost' can also mean 'penis'. I don't know whether George was aware of this double meaning, but I wouldn't put it past him.

TOWN

ALFRED PLACE/CORPORATION STREET

So this is it; town proper. On Alfred Place, you're on one of the little backstreets that warren Aberystwyth, more or less smack in the middle, if you take the sea itself as a compass point (which you should, really): West. Pretending that your first port of call is the Tourist Information Centre, cross Terrace Road between the off-licence and the Milk Bar, and you're on Corporation Street. Alfred Place adjoins.

You can hear gulls, and traffic, and crashing waves. Music from bedsits and pubs, outside the doors of which smokers lean and puff, this being the second week of the smoking ban in enclosed public spaces (and whichever open public spaces they don't want you to poison yourself in either). This is Aberystwyth. You can smell curry and fried chicken and exhaust and rotting weed on the nearby shore. William Dean Howells, the self-styled 'Cymric-fetched American', writes of the town in his bizarre little book *Seven English Cities*[1] that 'the long parade was filled at most hours with the English, who make the place their resort; whose bathing began early in the morning and whose flirting continued far into the night, with forenoon and after-noon dawdling and dozing on the pebbles'. He appears to have spent his time searching hopefully for elements of American culture in Aberystwyth, and his delight at the 'White Neegurs on the Terrace' is cringeworthy. He talks of a 'British Chautauqua', too, whatever that is, who 'had been invited to a gentleman's place not far from Aberystwyth to view as indubitable a remnant of the Holy Grail as now exists'[2]. The weather, he exclaims, is sunny. Children try to importune money from him through 'offerings of flowers and song'. He remarks that the local people 'might stand only five feet in their stockings, but they stood straight, and if they were respectful, they were first self-respectful.... In their manners [they] could not be more amiable than the English.... There was an absence of the cloying loyalty which makes sojourn in England afflictive to the republican spirit'. He writes that he sees no drunkenness, not even of a Saturday night – how things change – and that most of the English visitors were 'from the midland cities' – how they stay the same. Sightseers 'can do all the ordinary objects of interest... in half a day or half an hour', he writes, '[but] we had fallen in love with the place, and we would have fain stayed on after the week was up for which we had taken our lodging'.

So writes a Septic Tank in the, at a guess, late nineteenth century.

I imagine him in his topper and his muttonchop sideburns and his toothy grin (he's as obsessed with the state of Welsh dentition as he is with height) and with his earnest mannered politeness. What would he make of it now? He'd see things that would make the waxed ends of his muzzy uncurl, I'm sure. That would cause steam to whistle and hiss from his starched collar. That would lift the titfer off his head with a claxon sound.

Still, I like him. He's an innocent, adrift in the land of his fathers, and that's endearing (despite his hinted-at admiration for Cromwell, who wrecked Aber's castle, amongst a million other things), and of course his piece on Aber is a real insight into the life of the town a century or so ago (albeit filtered through the eyes of a travelling American). So, now that we're here, in the heart of the town in the heart of Wales on the very western edge of Europe, let's have a few more general introductions:

J. Geraint Jenkins, in his *Ceredigion: Interpreting an Ancient County*, writes that the town was originally called Llanbadarn Gaerog and only took on it's current name in 'Tudor times', and that between the erection of the castle in the thirteenth century and 'until the dawn of the eighteenth century, [it] was moribund both as a town and military establishment'. In 1763, though, the harbour was dredged, the bar across the entrance was drowned and the mining of lead and silver in the surrounding hills took off and the town's sea-trade expanded exponentially 'with imports of wines and spirits, bricks, slate and coal complementing the growing exports of lead ore, pickled herrings and oak bark'. The advent of the railway turned the town into a seaside resort, a 'rather brash' one for 'the industrial workers of southern Wales and the Midlands'. Brummagem again. Shipping declined, Beeching ripped up the railways, but the university was expanded and the National Library built and today Aberystwyth is 'very much an administrative, cultural and educational centre, but it still possesses many features that one associates with a seaside holiday'.

Fair enough. Michael Freeman in his *Aberystwyth: A History and Celebration* describes the town as 'an unusual [one] in many ways... little more than a small market and fishing village until English visitors began to come at the end of the 18th century'. Hmmm. Today he also sees it as 'a now thriving town with a vibrant culture [,] a cultural, social and administrative centre for much of mid-Wales', despite its car-parking problems, endemic to smallish towns with large hinterland catchment areas.

W.J. Lewis, who has perhaps written the definitive book on

Aberystwyth (albeit in need of a little up-dating now) in his exhaustively researched and indispensable *Born on a Perilous Rock*, isn't soundbite-able; the difficulty is in deciding what not to lift from his book, so absorbing and useful is it. His title alone serves, here, as an evocative introduction. And then there's the *Rough Guide*, with its 'salty blast of fresh air' etc., and the reeling Cornishman I once met drinking Special Brew on the beach at blazing noon who reckoned that 'there was no better place on the west coast to get pissed in'.

So, yes, you're in Aberystwyth. On Alfred Place. There's the Public Library, Edwardian, built in 1905 with a Carnegie Trust grant of £3,000. David Davies Llandinam laid the foundation stone, and the building was officially opened by Mrs. Vaughan Davies of Tanybwlch, wife of the then M.P. for Cardiganshire. A coach-builder's workshop was demolished to make room for the books. It's a handsome build-ing; designed by Paynton, whose interest in Art Nouveau is evident in the attractive green tiles in the lobby. And, of course, it's a useful building; William Howells (no relation to the American feller) keeps an extensive local history section. It's the place where I did my first public reading[3], from a short story published in a Parthian anthology (*Mama's Baby (Papa's Maybe)*, published in 1999). I had gout and couldn't stand.

There's Kane's pub, opposite the library on the corner, formerly the Unicorn Inn. Late Georgian. Last time I was in there, with Rocet Arwel Jones and Caryl Lewis[4], one of the toilet cubicles was shock-ingly awash in sick. Like an explosion in a soup factory; I've only witnessed a viler mess once, in Malmö in southern Sweden, when the explosion appeared to have taken place in a peanut butter factory. Or a Nutella one. Kane's barmaid cleared up the mess with extraordi-nary dexterity and efficiency; a mop and a bucket and some disinfectant and ten minutes later the place was sparkling, a pleasure to take a piddle in. I was impressed. Still am.

Opposite clean Kane's is the Italianate English Baptist Chapel, dating from 1870. Aber is full of these tucked-away temples, all of intriguing history; when this one was first opened, twenty two members of the Welsh Church were transferred to it to 'form a core of membership', to quote Lewis[5]. The first pastor, the Reverend T.E. Williams, served the chapel for two decades. During World War One, when 10,000 troops were billeted in Aberystwyth, the chapel school-room was used as a pay office, lecture room, quartermaster's store and rehearsal room. I've never been in it, but the outside's pretty enough. It's strongly independent (of course, being Baptist), but it retains its affiliation to other churches of similar denomination, not just in Aberystwyth. John Smyth[6,] I imagine, looks down with a little smile.

Behind the chapel are the Crynfryn Buildings, early nineteenth century cottages saved, thankfully, from demolition. Some close friends once lived there, and I've had some wondrous nights inside one of those tiny and snug cottages. They're built on a hill, which is proved by the stone steps that lead steeply down onto the promenade, often called the Hanging Steps, because condemned prisoners were led down there from the castle lych-gate to the gallows on the beach where now the bandstand, ahem, stands. These steps, too, have a vomit story; a friend was drunkenly descending them one night when he slipped and fell face-first into a pool of puke. In the morning he had a pain in his nostril. Blew his nose. Out came a half-digested chip. Just one more tale from the human heave in this not-quite-a-city place.

Off Alfred Place, on the corner of Eastgate and Baker Street, the Treehouse deli and café occupies Victoria House. Organic produce. Health-conscious eating. From 1870 to 1910 it was the Victoria Inn, and the ship's figurehead of the unamused queen that was once used as an inn-sign is still there, set into an alcove above the door. It's a rarity; carved in 1840, the only merchant ship figurehead of Victoria to have survived in Great Britain and, apparently, one of only four in the world. It almost faces yet another Baptist chapel, this time a Welsh one, built on a site of a block of four houses at a cost of £1,270 and designed

by Richard Owen of Liverpool, a relative of Hugh Owen who worked so hard to establish a Welsh university that his name is given to the Arts Centre building in the newer campus on Penglais Hill. The chapel was opened in 1878. During World War Two it was used as a school for evacuees from Liverpool, then as a centre for veterans of Dunkirk. The Reverend Pritchard disappeared from the chapel, and indeed Aberystwyth, and then the world, in May 1945. His body was found in the sea off Scarborough. Probable suicide.

The chapel turns away from the Varsity pub, on the corner of Upper Portland Street and Terrace Road. It was once the White Horse Hotel, a great and attractive hostelry, and whilst some of the original features still remain on the outside – the green glazed tiles, the engraved glass bow window (often smashed, and replaced at great expense) – on the inside, it's the same as any Varsity pub anywhere else in the country. Cheap food and two-for-one deals. Student favourite. The big windows give it a goldfish-bowl feel, but I prefer to sit looking out of them nonetheless because if you can't see Aberystwyth outside then, surrounded by decor replicated in the chain country-wide, you could be in Darlington. Or Portsmouth. Or Northampton Or Bedford or Leicester. I could go on but I won't. The drift's been got, I'm sure.

THE COLISEUM AND BATH STREET

See the stairs that lead into the building between the Officers Club (cheap clothing store) and the Tourist Information Centre? Go up them. They'll take you into The Coliseum, which houses the town's museum.

It's Tardis-like; surprisingly spacious inside. It was built in 1904 and has statues of Edward VIII crowning its three principal facades. The upper floors catered for theatre and music hall and public meetings and speeches, including some delivered by Lloyd George and Mrs. Pankhurst. It became a cinema in 1931 and the extravagant plushness of picture-houses in those days is still very much in evidence. It closed as a cinema in 1976 and has, since then, been the Ceredigion Museum. The ground floor, now occupied by Boots the Chemist and the aforementioned Officers Club, and, round the corner in Bath Street, a charity shop, was once a Cardiff-style shopping arcade; the mosaic floor of the Bath Street entrance recalls that function. And the Tourist Information Centre was formerly the town dwelling of Trawscoed's Vaughan family, the Lords Lisburne, wealthy land and mine owners. Now, it furnishes me with a leaflet telling me that the National Milk Bar over the road directly opposite has fenestration which 'illustrates the change in fashion in windows from Regency bow to Victorian bay'.

It's also an art gallery, The Coliseum, and I'm disappointed to find out that I've missed, by a mere day, Karen Pearce's exhibition 'Tref/Town'. Replacing it is a show of Celtic pipes and flutes by Alan Ginsburg (no, not that one), which, fascinating though it is, is no substitute. Bugger. Forthcoming exhibitions include a Guy Mahe retrospective (one of St. Brieuc's[7] 'most respected painters'), a 'War and Peace at Aberystwyth Castle'-themed show of mosaics (see the 'Castle' section later), 'Shout! The History of Lifeboats in Aberystwyth' (with a nod to Lulu), and 'Comfort Blankets: Contemporary Textiles by Becky Knight', although the promotional leaflet bears the sweet misprint 'texties'. Another flyer advertises the forthcoming Fancy Dress Halloween Ball at Nanteos mansion, featuring music by the Batmonkeys and the Mighty FUOD and Jape. I wonder if anybody went in a gimp mask, carrying a horsewhip with cuckold's horns glued to his head? Maybe a certain ghost did....

2005 was the centenary year of The Coliseum, so it was re-used, temporarily, as a theatre, hosting a film night of reels from the Screen and Sound Archive of the National Library with live piano accompaniment and a performance by Arad Goch of Jeremy Turner's *The Girl at Cae Bach*. Arad Goch, in fact, have a space on Bath Street, round the corner from The Coliseum; at the time of writing, it's being extensively renovated, thanks to Objective 1 funding. They're good, Arad Goch; they've earned the award.

I buy two booklets in the museum gift shop, both penned by the curator, Michael Freeman. One is a history of The Coliseum in pictures, including one from 1900 of the hall that stood here before The Coliseum and which burnt down on Boxing Day in 1902. Horses and carts and straw boaters and spats and cummerbunds and, in the foreground (the picture's taken from an elevated position, probably out of a window), the lanterns for the White Horse Hotel, which, as we know, is now the Varsity pub. It also contains pictures of a famous local actor of the 1920s, Ernest Chambers, in four costumes; he's in outrageous blackface for *The Geisha*. Fan and kimono and inscrutable smirk and everything. The other booklet is a guide to the museum's exhibits which opens with a noble declaration: 'Ceredigion Museum is a living mediator between the past and present. We aim to reflect the history of the county through material evidence'. It succeeds – there are currently 40,000 items in the permanent collection, remarkable for a county museum. The walls are covered in original paintings, many of a seafaring theme; it's impressed upon you in here how vital maritime activities have been to the growth and development of the town. Tourism, too; the collection of brochures and posters, designed to entice visitors, reminds me, a tad disquietingly, of the exhibition of Stalinist-era art I once visited in Gdansk; the sheer functionalism, the plain lines and primary colours, the smiling, cravatted and coiffed couples. I muse (appositely, considering where I am) on that similarity, but come to no conclusion. I'll give it a five-pint ponder at some later date.

Part of the exhibition concerns the rural poor. I'm drawn to it. There are original farm and domestic implements, like horrendous torture-devices, and photographs of wildly-bearded men in rags that you can almost smell. Shawled women, cheeks sunken through toothlessness. The myth of the cosy farm kitchen is debunked; it's there, to a degree, but the raw and mucky business of the life outside it is underlined. There is a quote on the wall from J.G. Jenkins, from his *Getting Yesterday Right*: 'It is far easier to arrange "Ye olde Welsh farm kitchen" complete with dresser, cradle, Bible and framed pictures of William Williams Pantycelyn than to present an authentic picture of poverty that characterised much of Welsh rural life'. These stabs at authentic representation are to be admired. Bucolic ideals, particularly when applied to Celtic countries, are Enlightenment, imperialist constructs, political propaganda; 'let's not worry about these people', they say, 'their lives are happy. They're at one with nature'. Phthisis and screwfly and crippling poverty and isolation and disease and trying to wrest vegetables from stones and an ingrained sense of duty to cross the mountain on a Sunday to be told that you're not doing enough to save your soul from eternal torment: these are not the ingredients of a simple, unworried existence. Look at the faces in the photographs, here. Look at the skin. The eyes.

I like this museum. It's a good place.

MARINE TERRACE (PROMENADE)

Ah, Marine Terrace. Promenade. Spinal column of the town. Central nervous system. Important things happen here; nerve-centres spark and fire to ganglions throughout the town, the county, the country.

Sometimes the sea hurls boulders up onto the paving. Sometimes the waves move cars. Porpoises leap, on occasion. Dark shapes move beneath the surface, now blue, now green, now grey, now silver. People watch this happening.

Start at the northern end, below Constitution Hill, by Alexandra Hall. On the sea-wall above the concrete steps that lead down to the pebbled beach is a horizontal bar, about thigh-high; this is the object of the 'Kicking the Bar' ritual, when strollers start at the harbour at the extreme southern end of the promenade and walk the entire length up to here, marking the end of their walk and putting a full-stop to their perambulation by kicking the bar. It's a practice that, frankly, I find a little embarrassing to witness. I don't know why. Rocet Arwel Jones[8] tells me that there are two theories as to its origins; one is that, when the recently renovated Alexandra Hall was a female-only dormitory, local boys invented the ritual as a reason to walk past the hall. The second is that, to combat TB, doctors invented it to goad people into walking. Both credible theories. But I still find the sight of people kicking that bar a wee bit cringeworthy.

Alexandra Hall is a mixed hall now, and has recently been re-opened after years of dereliction, when it looked as if the place was going to be allowed to crumble or be demolished to make way for a car park. I went in once, in its derelict days; the back doors had long been kicked in or ripped off. Floors had caved in. There was a stink of mould and several types of piss. The kitchens still had their huge ovens, now caked in greasy rust, and the ballroom still had its grand piano. Water dripped and formed deep slime-mantled pools and wind wailed through the broken windows. The impression was one of massive and irreversible decay, but the renovation has been monumental. The building's stonework is stunning; it's had brickies I know breathless with admiration. Behind it, Cliff Terrace with its handsome Edwardian townhouses turns into a private road which you can walk up to the crest of Constitution Hill. The town's old reservoir can be found up here; it's now a private, sunken garden.

It's impressive, the promenade, in the way it sweeps. Richard Cobb, in his little essay 'The View from the Promenade'[9], describes his despondency at moving to Aberystwyth from Paris in 1955 to take up a teaching post, and how he rapidly grew to love having, in his lectures, to compete with the noise of the sea and the wind and the gulls. He remarks, fascinatingly, on how a long promenade and three beaches affords a unique and perfect vantage point for social observation; how, from the parade next to the sea, the town's human traffic and commerce can be scrutinised. He's not wrong, even half a century on; people still tend to move seawards, dragging their baggage behind them. Directly outside Aber train station is a sign reading 'TRAETH', but really it should read 'MOR', because it's the ocean, not the earthy littoral, that attracts people. All that salty liquid.

Next to Alexandra Hall are yet more halls; one of them used to be the Seabank Hotel, but that burned down some years ago. Again, the renovation work has been painstaking. There's the Glengower Hotel, very much a student hang-out and consequently a place I don't frequent, although I've watched many a sunset slowly blur from the benches outside, facing the sea. Behind this, on Queens Road that runs parallel with the prom, the old Boar's Head pub stands crumbling. This was once a good and lively bar, popular with gays and thespians, with a big log fire and dance-club in the back room. It closed, and was taken over by the Po-na-na chain, whose pole-dancers caused apoplexy amongst the town elders, as would those of Clwb Yoko's, later. This advertised itself as a 'souk' bar, and so only served spirits and bottles, nothing on draft[10]. That, too, closed, and the building lay empty and boarded up until it was squatted and turned, unofficially of course, into the Plas y Bobl (the 'People's Palace'). I call round there one weekday afternoon with the same Alcohol Outreach worker I mentioned earlier and who will again be pseudonymously referred to as 'Steve'. 'Croeso' is painted above the door. Sheets of wood cover the windows like eyelids in slumber. The place has been boarded up for years.

Steve rings the bell and a dapper fellow answers the door. This is Bob Maycock, who came to Aber to be closer to his girlfriend, Jess, who is studying here. The interior of the building is a mess, but a clean and homely one; the inhabitants have carried out extensive remedial structural work and the place isn't falling apart anymore. It hosts parties, film nights, gigs, etc. It's been turned, again, into a useful, public space. The recent Latino night attracted 150 people, most crammed into the labyrinthine back room which has been recessed and grottoed and caved.

Bob is an experienced, activist squatter. There's a political point to what he does, and it offered him a sort of salvation after he lost his job and home a few years ago. A French graffiti artist, met in France, had visited Aberystwyth and recommended the Boar's Head to Bob as ripe for squatting so Bob had his legal men (oh yes – this is a serious, well-organ-

ised business) do a search and found that there was a question mark concerning ownership hanging over the building, so Bob and his people visited and assessed. The French doors were open so entry was made without breaking; the building had been used by street-drinkers, glue-sniffers, chronic alcoholics who needed a place to drink after the ban on public imbibing came into force and drug and drink detritus was scattered everywhere (including, it must be said, mounds of excrement). So Bob and his people transformed the place; restoring running water and electricity, painting and furnishing it, generally making it habitable. He's very keen, Bob, to stress the positivity of this act, and I'm in no way inclined to disagree. He's at pains to keep drug use out of the building because that would offer ammunition to those who want to shut it down and the police have, in general, been supportive, and not obstructive in any way. 'They don't really get it', Bob says, 'but they've been good to us'.

I ask him how long he expects to be here and he says 'they'll have to remove me physically'. He has a publicity machine behind him in the form of various websites and radio stations and an alternative local newspaper called the *Cambrian Snooze* which appears intermittently and can be picked up, for free, from various pubs and wholefood emporia etc. around the town. The first edition, from April 2006, declares that it is 'a genuinely independent, radical, alternative newspaper, with a social conscience, an eye for a story, and a sense of humour', and its front page carries an article about the Social Forum Cymru events, basically a carnival of protest supported by no less a personage than Noam Chomsky. Later editions dissect student apathy, and how that was disproved, on one occasion, by the large demonstrations over lecturer's wage-strikes; and another carried an interview with Moazzam Begg, a one-time Guantanamo Bay detainee who spoke at the Social Forum Cymru. It's become a vital and valid ingredient of the town's cultural life; a part of that alternative undercurrent which makes up much of the town's attractiveness. It's still going, the *Cambrian Snooze*, despite the eviction of the squatters in late 2006, when they dressed up as clowns and hid from the bailiffs in the building's warren of rooms and corridors. It was a peaceful eviction; the only angry voices belonged to those homeless people who staged a protest-within-a-protest, accusing the Plas y Bobl crew of being the offspring of rich parents, and merely playing at squatting. I can't comment on that, even if I wanted to; I know very little about the Plas y Bobl cast. The squatters were ordered to pay £1,500 in court costs and, over a year later, the Boar's Head is, once again, an empty, crumbling, useless shell. The Plas y Bobl people have moved on. The Boar's Head just rots, and maybe it'll continue to do so until it has interest only for archaeologists, like the odd network of rooms and cavities that was unearthed in 2005 beneath a building next to the Belle Vue hotel that was being converted into flats. They maybe formed part of the old town walls, but investigators disagreed, and a consensus was never reached. So they were simply built on. They're still there. Under the flats. Phantom-inhabited places. We create more of them every day.

Siop y Prom; Bay Hotel; Richmond Hotel. Look at the benches that form a dotted line the entire length of Marine Terrace; the metal struts that support the wooden seats are moulded in the form of snakes, complete with forked and flickering tongues. Alfred, Lord

Tennyson stayed at the Belle Vue, where he wrote: 'this place, the Cambrian Brighton, pleases me not'[11]. Maybe he could feel the vile vibrations from the tumulus behind the hotel, known as Penbryn-dioddef, or the Hill of Suffering, once the site of a whipping post and gallows, now a set of houses on Albert Place.

The King's Hall Carvery, occupying part of the ground

floor of the posh block of white veranda'd flats, is worth a mention. It was first built in the 1820s; before that it was part of the Morfa Swnd, or Sand Marsh[12]. Private dwellings were erected first; in 1890 these were knocked through to form the Waterloo Hotel, ran as a Temperance institute and also as a Hydro, offering electrical and sea-water treatments to many a Mr. Pooter afflicted by a surfeit of the bilious humour brought on by too close an examination of a piano leg. Just after World War One, the whole building burnt down[13] and the site effectively lay empty until 1933 when work began on the Municipal Hall and Palm Court, soon re-named the King's Hall after George V visited in 1935. It was a huge space with a capacity of hundreds and a bumper-boat pond in the basement. Gilbert and Sullivan operas were performed there, as were gymnastic shows, and in the 1970s names as big as The Rolling Stones and Led Zeppelin and (of course) Tom Jones appeared[14]. The inevitable neglect and slide into disrepair came in the 1980s, and demolition of the suppos-edly dangerously unsound building took two years. Briefly the site was used as a car-park until re-development began in 1991, and now it's a caff and retail space below three levels of private accommoda-tion with a paved open public apron with a few benches and a sculpture of a standing open book and an information point and many a pigeon on the scrounge.

Phinnikki's, the snack bar, stands opposite, on the side of the prom nearest the sea. Ice cream and burgers and baguettes and chrome-tubing tables and chairs under big umbrellas and the bigger sky. I meet Carwyn Fowler here, who you've already encountered. Carwyn works for *Golwg* magazine and he impresses upon me the importance of the promenade to the Welshness of Aberystwyth; indeed, the offices of Cymdeithas yr Iaith are located on Marine Terrace, opposite the pier, between the two Chinese take-aways and the Olive Branch Greek restaurant. Carwyn was born in Leicester, a descen-dant of the Liverpool Welsh on his mother's side, and moved to Borth at the age of ten. He's working on a research project under the umbrella title of 'Aberystwyth and the Reproduction of Nationalism' and which is part-funded by the Board of Celtic Studies (annexed to the National Library) and by Carwyn's own busking on the Celtic harp, which he learned by ear. His political awakening came at a young age and he became a member of Cymdeithas yr Iaith at fourteen. He resides in Cardiff now but, for both research and recre-ational purposes, spends a lot of time in Aberystwyth. What is it about the town, I ask him, which throws him a little because he's recently been asking the same question of others. 'From an institutional point of view', he says, 'Aber is equally inconvenient for everyone', which makes me laugh. He talks about the town's café culture, and how important that's been for the growth of language politics (see 'Trefechan', qv.). I lob the word 'Abercuawg' at him. 'It's not that,' he says, 'but it is a microcosm of Wales in many ways. You can't think of Aber without thinking of social class, for example the housing estates of Penparcau looking out over the town, the 'Surrey' of Dan y Coed [which makes me laugh again].... Here, there is Cymraeg Wales, rural Wales, a non-Welsh- speaking population.... I'm not romanticising it, but it is a microcosm'.

I hear Ned Thomas echoed here and am impressed by the unifying themes and threads that can be traced throughout the individual activisms I've so far encountered. The truth in Carwyn's statement, that 'strength of nationalism is a unifying tool for political purposes', is clear.

Can Aber retain its Welshness? It is a protean place. Can it keep a grounded identity? It can do more than that, Carwyn replies (and I paraphrase); it reproduces the Welsh character. It's no longer only a fishing port, but a university town, a political centre, with an array of subcultures. Aberystwyth people re-define themselves continually.

I like that; it's one of the most upbeat and optimistic comments on the town that I hear. Carwyn leaves to continue his researches and I proceed further down the promenade. There's a breeze blowing, and the minority flags are set flapping. These are a series of standards representing the minority nations and/or languages of Europe with their names on the poles in their own language, English, and Welsh. There's Wales, of course, Ireland, Scotland, Cornwall, Isle of Man, Occitania, the Basque country, the Tyrol, Latvia, and many more. Baner y Butler, they're called, in honour of Gareth Butler who first had the idea and campaigned for its realization in 1991. Carwyn, in his unpublished (at the time of writing) essay 'Crud Cenedlaetholdeb Gymraeg/A Cradle of Welsh Nationalism', quotes Sion Jobbins on these flags: 'this is what creates an alternative reality to Britishness, the flags are something that everybody notices'. They're more important than that, even; in a Welsh town where the Cross of St. George or the Union Jack is often flown from the windows of halls of residence or from car aerials, baner y Butler are necessary tonics to that arrogance and smirking imposition. Simon Rodway, a teacher of Welsh in the university's Celtic Studies Department (and in a private capacity, too), writes in his unpublished (again, at the time of writing)

article 'Flag Waving' that the history of Britain is a history of antago-
nistic relationships, that the history of Wales 'is not that of brave
longbow-men at Crecy and Agincourt or of Lady Llanover and her
stove-pipe hats; it is Hywel Dda and Llywelyn, the Blue Books and
the Welsh Not, Saunders Lewis and Tryweryn.... [England] is not [a]
partner in the made-up state of Great Britain.... To fly the flag of St.
George in Wales is different only in degree from flying the Russian
flag in Poland'.

I've heard similar sentiments expressed in Poland itself. And
whenever the flags are taken in for cleaning, the promenade seems
glaringly empty, too big and bare. It doesn't matter if the tourists at
Phinikki's tubular tables don't look up from their bowls of chips; the
fact that the flags fly is all that counts.

It's dusk, and I sit in the shelter by the pier to watch the starlings
fly in to roost. Scores of thousands of them gather each night on the
barnacle-encrusted beams and struts. They fill the sky, they move like
oil collectively, diving and swooping and suddenly funnelling into the
dank space beneath the salty slats. The noise under there is deafen-
ing, but a unique experience (be sure to take an umbrella, however).
Fierce spotlights were once installed under there to keep the birds
and their corrosive emissions away, but they had no effect whatsoever
and still the starlings come, swirling, plummeting clouds of them. If
you sit in the pier brasserie at dusk, it can be as if you're part of that
astonishing flock; you join the mad fluttering blizzard. Only thin glass
separates you. At sundown, a dark car parked on Marine Parade by
the pier or Old College will, in seconds, become a Dalmatian dog.

Matt Francis, another Aber-resident poet, has written about the
birds in his brilliant volume *Whereabouts*, a collection of thirty-five
pieces, each a forty-five syllable sestet, declining in length from
thirteen syllables in the first line to four in the last. Each piece enacts
a sense of homing in, of a kind of distillation. The poem is called
'Starlings', it's perfect, and here it is:

> The day is on the turn. The evening is flying home
> in waves of dark, shapeshifting at a twitch
> of its shared REM mind,
>
> settling out of the air
> on to the flutter
>
> of the thronged roost.

WATER: THE RHEIDOL

Aberystwyth is built on water. The sea is obvious, but the two rivers that push the town towards it make sure that water remains the blood of the place, dictating the heartbeat, causing the pulse. The Ystwyth river gives the town its name of course, and we'll take a dip in that one later, but right now let's stand where the Rheidol begins, on the slopes above Cwmystwyth, the wind-blasted moonscapes leftover from the mining enterprises that ripped and gouged these hills. See that wee spring, just about discernible, a bubble in the bog? That's the Rheidol. You're on Bryn Garw[15], specifically at Banc Nant Rhys, 2,003 feet above sea level, and the trickle of the Rheidol will, further down the steep slope tussocked with rye grass and squishy with quag, join the even smaller rivulet threading down from Cae Gaer and form one larger waterway above the Llywernog lead mine just outside Ponterwyd, on the slopes of Pumlumon at 2,469 feet. You're up high. The rivers have climbed. The Rheidol will kineticise itself at Parson's Bridge and join with the Mynach to churn and thunder through Devil's Bridge and smash itself and re-form on the valley floor where it will, after a series of white-water rapids[16], wind through a secluded, wooded valley[17], below and between old mine workings on the valley sides stubbled with ruins and shaded orange by the slag, rising up past and over waterfalls and minute villages. It's beautiful, the Rheidol valley. In the right weather conditions, it can stun. It passes below Aberffrwd and gets held up for a minute at the Cwmrheidol hydro-electric dam and then meanders through Capel Bangor and Llanbadarn Fawr and becomes the sea at Aberystwyth harbour,

below Pen Dinas. The Vale of Rheidol steam train will follow the river back and forth between Aberystwyth and Devil's Bridge stations, but if you've time and stamina and health enough, a walk along at least a stretch of it is unbeatable. What will you see? Dragonflies and ram's horn snails and caddis flies and various amphibians and bullhead and loach and brown trout and watercress and water plantain and crowfoot and stitchwort. What might you see? Sewin, if you're lucky, swimming sea-wards to spawn, crayfish if you take time to lift rocks, and, if you're very still and quiet and depending on what time of day it is, voles and shrews and mink and maybe even otter; they've returned to both of Aber's rivers in recent years. Plus herons and dippers and wagtails and reed warblers and buntings. Maybe a kingfisher, like a flash of the rainforest in the mid-Welsh green. What won't you see? Litter and dogshit and farting vehicles. The river's name echoes the Welsh word 'rheidiol', and might, in fact, be from that, meaning in English 'necessary' or 'needful'. Say no more.

THE OLD COLLEGE AND LAURA PLACE

It's another hot day when I explore the leaning narrow streets between South Road/harbour and Laura Place/Old College. Doors and windows have been opened and flower pots and hanging baskets are in bloom. There's colour and music everywhere, good music too – I hear Dylan from one house and some fine wailing woebegone country stuff from another. No Elton or Phil or Robbie within earshot, thank Christ. People are smiling, and it's not yet April. What's going on? The pavement is being dug up between the Ship and Castle pub and the Merched y Wawr building. I spend an hour or so scouring the packed shelves in Ystwyth Books, as I often like to do (it's a treasure chest for an avid reader), then mosey to the promenade, stopping to chat on the way with Simon Rodway, and Pete, who's contracted gout and is limping, so we swap gouty tales for a bit. I tell him that allopurinol is a great drug for treating the condition; it doesn't suit everybody, but if it does, you can be gout-free. I haven't had an attack in years. At the moment Pete's on indomethacin, an anti-inflammatory, which gets rid of the gout but replaces it with terrible stomach cramps, in my experience. Pete hobbles off and I meet Keith Morris on the prom (you'll meet him later). Keith's a professional photographer. His camera's much, much bigger than mine.

I skirt Castle Point and tut because the kiosk opposite the end of South Road is shut. Could've done with a cheese roll and a cup of tea. The southern sea-cliffs fade away into a silvery haze. I turn up Sea View Place and turn left at the Theatr y Castell into Laura Place. A terrace of Regency housing built between 1810 and 1820. A little along the adjoining New Street is a curious white and blue building in a state of some disrepair; it served, apparently, as the meeting house of the Unitarians and Quakers. The grand building at the top of Laura Place with the Venetian windows is the old Assembly Rooms, built by George Repton in 1820, a place where gentlemen and ladies could gather to cut a dash. At the turn of the last century it served as the university college chemistry department and, after that, as the first home of the National Library of Wales. It remained the Student's Union between 1923 and 1970 and is now the Extra Mural department. The first floor hosts chamber concerts and is named the Joseph Parry Hall, in honour of the composer who was professor of music here between 1874 and 1880 and whose lovely hymn 'Aberystwyth' can often be heard from the Ship and Castle just before chucking-out time.

The Extra Mural department, as it was, saw the beginnings of the Urdd Gobaith Cymru (the 'Welsh Order of Hope'), another Aber-based development whose importance in the creation of contemporary Welsh identity cannot be overstated. Ifan ab Owen Edwards graduated from UWA and left Wales for several years; on his return, the decline of interest and confidence in all things Welsh dismayed him. Whilst teaching at Dolgellau Grammar School he was invited by Principal J.H. Davies of Aberystwyth to join the staff of the university Extra Mural department. He accepted, and during his tenure, whilst lodging in Llanarth, he wrote an article for the publication *Cymru'r Plant* ('Children of Wales') that appealed to Welsh children to join together to create the Welsh League of Youth, or the 'Urdd', as a way of preserving Welsh language and identity. The response was a keen one and the *Cronicl yr Urdd* magazine was set up, which, within a few months, was distributing 30,000 copies. This was in 1922, the year that Ifan got married and moved to Llanuwchlyn, whose post office was too small to cope with the volume of mail addressed to the Urdd. The answer to this problem seemed to lie in de-centralisation, so various camps were set up around the country, all of which came together at one place in the summer months[18]. In 1929 the first Urdd Eisteddfod was held, and in the 1930s Sir Ifan, as he had become, moved back to Aberystwyth, where Salisbury House on Llanbadarn Road became the Urdd Headquarters, as it is still. The Urdd's aims are to engender a sense of Welsh citizenship amongst young people, and anyone under twenty-five can join as long as s/he promises to adhere to the pledge of service to Wales, to one's fellow man, and to Christ (this last has led to fierce criticism of the Urdd in some quarters for being too dogmatic). The movement remains extremely popular; twenty years ago it had 12,000 branches and

62,000 members[19], and it's grown exponentially since then. Most of its costs are met by the Welsh citizenry. Ifan will always be spoken of in princely terms.

Which adjective allows me to segue, not too awkwardly, into the Old College, whose Old Boys include Ol' Big Ears himself, Noddy's mate, Charlie Boy, the Principality's un-elected Prince (or 'Charlo' as the youthful Paul Henry called

him); HRH the Prince of Wales, Charles Saxeburg-Gotha-Windsor (or whatever his full name is). He studied here in the late 1960s, as did (albeit at different times) Gwynfor Evans M.P. and the great poet-activist Waldo Williams. Illustrious alumni indeed. The building began as a hotel; in 1864, the year the railway reached Aber, Thomas Savin bought Castle House, a castellated mansion designed by John Nash, and commissioned J.P. Seddon, a distinguished Gothic revival-ist of the time, to incorporate it into the luxurious Castle Hotel. Seddon added a central towered block and northern wing to the existing structure but Savin went bankrupt in 1866 and the unfin-ished hotel was bought, cheaply, by the organisation that was to become the University College of Wales. Again, this was a hugely important gesture, and one central to the growth of Welsh identity. Ben Bowen Thomas, in his *'Aber': 1872-1972*, describes how a group of (largely) London Welshmen campaigned for the establishment of a Queen's College for Wales in much the same way as colleges had been set up in Ireland. One of the biggest obstacles they found was the apathy of the Welsh populace; nonconformist ministers and clergy had St. David's College Lampeter to worry about; the landed gentry were, true to form, indifferent to the edificatory needs of the common citizens; the new industrialists were characterised by a trait of philis-tinism; and the working men, beyond their chapels and churches, in the main saw no benefit in a university, and the few who did were unorganised and lacking in leadership. By 1863, though, Hugh Owen had grown tired of this and so sought to galvanize the Welsh public into supporting the setting up of a university; he succeeded, money was raised, and the College opened its doors on 16 October 1872, a

day which was declared a public holiday in Aberystwyth. There were only three members of staff, the principal (the Revd. Thomas Charles Edwards, of Liverpool), and twenty-six students, but it was a beginning. W.J. Lewis, in *Perilous Rock,* points out how difficult the first few years were; the struggle was with not only money shortages but with failings of imaginative sympathy, too, as 'every' public and religious body in Wales sought to find fault to the extent that the principal was lambasted by Calvinists for attending an athletics match in, Heaven forfend, 'broad daylight'. Impecuniousness was the worst threat, however; an appeal to the Treasury was turned down, even though similar financial help had been given to universities in both Scotland and Ireland. The general populace had begun to contribute, but it wasn't enough, and only the tireless government lobbying seemed to work when, in 1882, Aberystwyth received a grant of £4,000, which was diverted to Bangor after it was decided in Chester that that was a better-placed college to serve north Wales (Cardiff, of course, served the south). The MPs Stuart Rendel and David Davies Llandinam, admirably unfazed by the continuing farce, then intervened and pressed for support until the government yielded and agreed to give Aberystwyth £2,500 a year. Rendel remained unsatisfied and continued to press for £4,000 which, in 1885, he got.

Then came the fire. Flames gutted the north wing. The damage was estimated at over £20,000. Three firemen were killed. The university seemed finished, and it was then that the great wave of public contributions and support began to swell, as befitted 'one of the few genuinely popular universities in Europe', to quote Gwyn A. Williams in *When Was Wales?* The main governmental funding was won after the fire, prompted by the huge level of popular support and part-engineered by the network of Old Boys well-placed to work the system from within. And so it grew. By the late 1890s, more land was required. The College coughed some of itself out and it landed halfway up Penglais Hill, but we'll get to that later.

It's an impressive structure, both metaphorically and literally. 'Not

Wales for the Welsh, but Wales for the world', said Principal Roberts, famously, but the university is seen, primarily, as a uniquely Welsh success story, a confirmation of the confidence in Welsh identity and culture that re-asserted itself in the late 1800s (it was to fade away again, for a while, but that's another story). Marcus Tanner, in his brilliant and emotive *The Last of the Celts*, points out that much of the initial money for the enterprise was supplied by quarrymen, despite, or probably because of, the Anglicised gentry's boycotting of the college, and that 'University Sunday' collections in the chapels made the act of raising funds a patriotic crusade.

The building glows almost golden in the setting sun. Pretty mosaic murals on the southern tower look down over the castle ruins and the crazy golf course. The internal quadrangle of the college has repro-duction statues in it of Lord Aberdare, First President of the College, and of Thomas Edward Ellis M.P. The atmosphere, particularly inside, is one of determined devotion, in all manner of things. This is pleasant, in its way, although the hint of crusty discipline and the disapproval that usually accompanies that taints it a tad. Yet a visit to the building always seems to have the effect of making me want to read more and write more and study more and achieve more. But not wearing a cloak.

ST. MICHAEL'S AND GRAVEYARD

Facing the Old College is St. Michael's Church and its accompanying cemetery (and attached car park, often the only place to leave your car on a Saturday; traffic congestion in the town is severe). Michael Freeman, in his *Aberystwyth: A History and Celebration*, points out that the church is built on the highest part of the town, and his panorama taken from the vantage point of the National Library proves it; the spire surfaces from the surrounding jumble of roofs, a whale amongst minnows. It's a big, imposing structure; I've heard that, were Aber ever to achieve city status, this would be consecrated as a cathedral. It would do, I guess – I've seen smaller – but it would be dwarfed next to the cathedral in, say, St. David's, or Ely, or Lichfield, or Wells (towns with a similar size population to Aber). It makes for a magnificent church but would be a decidedly underwhelming cathedral. So what would happen, with citification? I don't know. Maybe a new edifice would go up. Maybe they'd hollow out Pen Dinas.

Early post-Reformation Aberystwyth had no place of worship at all; that was at Llanbadarn, two miles away, as we have seen, at that time over difficult-to-traverse marshland. The castle held a chapel to serve the spiritual needs of the garrison but that fell into desuetude, and another one built at Castle Point appears to have crumbled into the sea (see next section). A petition of 1762 stated that: 'We know of no town in Great Britain so large and populous as this, and yet so distant from a Church, and all its inhabitants, without exception, of the Established Church of England'. It then goes on to elicit funding from the townspeople, unsuccessfully, prompting the Reverend David Peters, Principal of Carmarthen Presbyterian College, to remark that 'the town of Aberystwyth [is] the seat of ignorance and vice'(many would say it still is), but a group of townsfolk did combine to buy a farm at Llancynfelyn, the income from which was used to endow the empty building by the castle and consecrate it in honour of St. Michael and All Angels. The baptismal register here opens on New Year's Day 1788 and that of burials on 16th August 1791 with the internment of 'Twiddy Twiddy, Player's Child'[20] .

The first church was small – sixty feet by twenty-six, although this was seen as adequate. But the town was expanding rapidly, and the area surrounding the church becoming rapidly exclusive and desirable, and this, added to the ecclesiastical zeal of the Rev. John Hughes of Llwyn Glas, led to the building of the second St. Michael's, begun at the receipt of a grant in 1825. Design work was entrusted to Edward Heycock of Shrewsbury, who, with an eye on ambient continuity, mixed simple Classical with Gothic, but it was badly constructed, and undermined by damp, so much so that the walls and furnishings were often coated with mould.

So work began on a third church, the land for which was presented by the Powells of Nanteos (yes, them again). This time, the designer was from Hereford – Nicholson and Son. Work began in 1894 when Heycock's church was pulled down. This third church still stands. It's Anglican, with some Welsh services, but the main Gymraeg church stands on Gray's Inn Road, off Bridge Street, another of Aber's hidden temples, on land donated by who else but Colonel Powell.

Its situation within a car park means that St. Michael's is often ignored, or unseen; you don't focus on diurnal routine, you work on autopilot – you park your car, pay your quid, and bugger off. You tend not to look at what's around you. But it's a grand and attractive structure, an echo of the Old College nearby in colour and castellation. It's well worth a gawp. As is the surrounding graveyard, some stones of which are banked up at a forty-five-degree angle on the levee that separates the car park from the green space abutting the castle grounds. These headstones and monuments were moved in 1977 in an act described as 'a ruthless exhibition of graveyard clearance', and that it was, but of course the dead do speak to the quick, and this shifting facilitated historical discovery and the 500 existing memorials illustrate the range of occupations of nineteenth century Aberystwyth, most of them, unsurprisingly, connected with the sea and shipping (conspicuous, too, is the high level of infant mortality). In the south-western corner of the necropolis, a stone bears the following legend:

JAMES
youngest son of the above named
JOHN AND MARY WILLIAMS
who met his untimely death by a
shot fired from a French war vessel
off Belle Isle, Bay of Biscay
on Sunday the 24th day of May 1857
Aged 21 years

Lionel Fanthorpe, the Fortean singing clergyman, in his book *Talking Stones*, discusses how young James Williams became the focal point of an international incident. In the 1850s, England and France were not, oddly, at war, but there was a blockade, and the French navy were insisting that all ships approaching Belle Isle flew their national colours. James's ship wasn't doing that, so an intended warning shot was fired, which struck young James as he was climbing the rigging to unfurl the Union Jack. He fell with the flag wrapped around him. He was buried on Belle Isle but both Wales and London protested; Lewis Llewellyn Dillwyn, Liberal MP for Swansea, brought the matter up in the Commons – what an affront not only to this young man's life but also to Her Majesty's Navy, he said. Strong emotions were rigorously stirred and the French captain responsible for James's death was court-martialled and a red-faced French navy returned James's body to Wales, the man-o-war that bore his coffin anchoring in Cardigan Bay on 1st August, 1857, observed by thousands. The coffin was brought ashore and buried with great solemnity in St. Michael's, amongst the Williams family plots.

And then a century later it was moved a few yards to make way for a new car park. There used to be a flat fee of fifty pence for use of this car park, deposited into a rusty honesty box. An attendant replaced that, and charged a quid. Now there's a 'PAY & DISPLAY' ticket machine. If you're lucky enough to get a space, that is.

CASTLE AND CASTLE POINT

The southern end of Aberystwyth is, more or less, a giant fortress; there's Pen Dinas, an iron-age redoubt, and of course the castle itself, and there were probably, at various times, various castley things in between. They were, and are, effective in repelling and protecting flesh and bone, our soft bodies, but there are mightier assailants – gravity, and time, and weather's relentless artillery. The castle walls, sodden and wind-hit, slowly become friable; each year someone tries to climb the still-standing central tower and falls to splintered bones or worse. And the legend persists of the chapel that once stood on Castle Point, in which makeshift marriages of the Gretna Green or Las Vegas type were conducted until the waves – unleashed by a displeased deity, no doubt – undermined it and its cemetery and sucked them down into the sea. Human bones and small pieces of

jewellery are still to be found in the sand, and when repairs were being made to Mount Pleasant House some time ago, whole skeletons and rotted coffins were unearthed. Similar finds were made under the main entrance to the College. A skull containing a bird's nest was found on the beach. The fluttering within that carapace did not end in death. Nor does the vanishing end; in October 2005,

Aberystwyth sea-front was listed as one of the 100 British features our grandchildren may never see, along with the nightingale, red telephone boxes, and pearl mussels, if global warming predictions come true (as they are appearing to do). This prompted the novelist Malcolm Pryce to remark: 'There is no doubt we will be losing something that can never be replaced. It's hard to imagine humanity ever doing bandstands and piers again'[21].

He's right, and that's terribly sad. Malcolm's novels themselves seem to recall a lost moment; their protagonist, Louie Knight, seems a product of a sadly gone age, more easily described as 'innocent' than our own, when a basic decency had a say in human affairs and dignity was something to aim for. The fantastic and humorous flavours of the novels, to Malcolm's credit, are not allowed to mask their darkly elegiac centres. Take this passage – or, rather, a conflation of two passages – from his first novel, *Aberystwyth Mon Amour*:

> If you walk south past the Pier and the Bandstand [and the twenty-four-hour whelk stall] you come to Castle Point where the Promenade turns sharply as if on a hinge. After that the town takes on a different character; an exposed, wind-beaten strip leading down to the harbour with a down-at-heel air.... The paving slabs, like flowers opening at dusk, started to release the distinctive perfume of the summer night... heavier tones of fried onions, spilled beer and the salty tang of sun-dried sea-weed; and on top of that coconut oil, sweat, spilled ice-cream, cheap aftershave and dog piss. It was a smell that belonged to the overhead lights...; a smell which would always be linked in the photo album of the soul with three particular sounds: The muted roar of the sea; the electronic chimes of the amusement arcades; and the demented banshee wail of the police sirens.

Malcolm hasn't lived in Aberystwyth for years; he resides in the Far East where, in fact, he conceived the idea for his series of Aber-themed books[22]. Aberystwyth's promenade is very, very long.

But, anyway, the castle. Paeans are important and interesting but aren't in themselves much of a guide, are they? William Dean Howells, in his *Seven English Cities*[23], gets all gushy about the ruins: 'One of those castles which the Normans planted with a mailed fist at every vantage in Wales, as their sole means of holding down the swarming, squirming, fighting little dark people of the country. Even they could not do it, for the Welsh, often overrun, were never conquered...'[24]. Here's the potted history:

It was one of the eight huge fortresses built by Edward I between

1277 and 1295 to keep his conquests safe from Llewelyn ap Gruffydd, the last native Prince of Wales. Edward's brother, Edmund of Lancaster, began the work in 1277 but it was still unfinished in 1282 when it was captured in a Welsh uprising. That was repelled within a few months, and work resumed, and the final stone was put in place in 1289. Like that at Harlech, the castle's location was part of its strength; provisionable by sea, it could withstand long land sieges, as it did for a year in 1294-1295, and again in 1401 during the Glyndŵr rebellion, although it fell to Owain in 1404 and had to be retaken in two stages in 1407 and 1408 by Henry V who needed to utilise bombardment by cannon. During the Civil War it was held for King Charles until it was surrendered to Parliamentary forces in 1646; three years later it was effectively ruined through mining and tunnelling to such a scale that it's difficult, today, to discern the original design; it was, apparently, concentric, roughly rhomboid, with two lines of towered walls and a strongly defended entrance at the east. The approach was barred by a barbican, and ditches hacked into the rock gave further protection. Much of the outer ward, except for the western corner, remains, but most of the inner ward has gone, long broken up to provide stones for the houses roundabout, or is now just humps of fallen masonry.

The cost of its construction ran to £4,300[25], much of it raised through English taxation[26] laws of jaw-dropping insensitivity (hence the first rebellion). Four roads branched out from it in directions roughly coterminous with compass points; one ran from the entrance to Great Darkgate Street, one ran to a bridge over the Rheidol, another went west to the town wall and the last to a gate that gave access to the beach. These four roads and the castle at their hub were, really, the entire town.

The castle has a well, sixty feet deep, discovered in 1844. Excavations between 1975 and 1988 revealed a large mural tower and the huge hall, which housed the royal mint set up by Thomas Bushell in 1637. This used silver from local mines and turned out coins of eight denominations, specimens of which can be seen in the town museum.

The stones that now stand in the inner courtyard are the circle of Gorsedd Stones; Aberystwyth has hosted the National Eisteddfod in 1865, 1916, 1952 and 1992. They number thirteen, to represent the counties of Wales pre-1974, and have the county names carved into them in bardic lettering. Small but lively music festivals are periodically held here, called, unsurprisingly, Castle Rock. Well attended, riotously good-natured affairs, showcasing local bands like Radio Luxembourg. Health and Safety issues, as usual, forced their temporary cessation, but at the time of writing they're about to resume, much to some people's chagrin. The Calvinists who attacked the Old College's first principal for watching athletics in daylight would've been proud.

On Castle Point stands one of Aber's war memorials. It was designed by Mario Rutelli in 1923 (and, of course, added to twenty two years later). The top statue, Winged Victory, carries a triumphal wreath and an olive branch; the bottom one, Humanity, is a nude female figure symbolising humanity freeing herself from war, and I've been told that she was modelled on the lady who owned Ernie's chip shop on Portland Road (now gone); if this is true, then she evidently didn't avail herself of her wares. She's... well, have a look at her. She prompted Matt Francis, in *Whereabouts*, to write this:

BRONZE ANGEL

Too flighty to stay long, she dips a toe in the world
and is off in a shimmer of nightgown,
a kerfuffle of feathers,

leaving behind only
a brazen wingbeat

impressed in air

Set into the stone wall beneath the memorial that follows Castle Point around to South Road are a series of mosaics depicting various events in Aberystwyth's history. They're beautiful artefacts, the work of Stuart Evans and Pod Clare (great name), who worked with nine local community groups. They won two awards for these mosaics, from the Interpret Britain and Ireland Awards, presented by odd-

voiced ex-professional nosey parker Loyd Grossman[27]. They succeed in making history available; in them, past events are shown to be quick, still, in their echoes and ramifications, that we are not dropped from nowhere, that the environment that shapes us was in turn, shaped by others (would that all public art aspired to this). I favour the depiction of the skeleton, or of Glyndŵr's ship, or of the Welsh capture of the castle. They suggest old tapestries in their clean jumble, but with perspective. Be careful if you sit on the benches in the recesses beneath each one, however; like the setback seats at the foot of Plas Crug, they almost touch the road (which can get very busy here in the summer months). Stretch out your legs and you might lose 'em.

If the kiosk's open, stop there for a cup of tea, and gaze at the sea before you double back into the castle. See the freestanding brick shed between the playground and Sea View Place? It's a public toilet, and, as Patty Duncker has written, 'the Castle cottage'[28]. It's to be closed, due to, so they say, budgetary concessions, so if you're at the south end of the prom and you're caught short you'll have to leg it to the grim little urinous cave next to the Sailing Club (but don't read the graffiti). Or take a dip in the sea. I've been propositioned in this cottage myself – a greasy crimson penis flopping out of a pair of shiny shellsuit bottoms is not my cup of tea – and I find it pleasingly ambiguous that this trysting-place for the sexually innovative should be situated here, amongst these symbols of militarism and subjuga-tion, mortared with testosterone, as all such places are[29]. Which is precisely why, now and here, I'll address Aber's unofficial standing as the 'gay capital of Wales' (and because a small Gay Pride march was once held in the castle grounds, probably for the same reason).

Mike Parker will be our guide here, as he is to much of Wales, being a co-author of the excellent *Rough Guide*. I meet him in Y Cŵps pub, before the renovation, in spring of 2006. We sit beneath the telly; Celtic are playing Hearts, and if they win they'll win the SPL. I have a soft spot for them, so I hope they do. Mike's from the Midlands originally, which, as he says, 'has an umbilical link with mid-Wales'.

He first came to Aberystwyth, like me, as a child, but his visits were directly aimed here, not diversions to pick up travel-sickness pills on the route to somewhere else. 'Wales was the horizon', he says, and he'd visit whenever he could. He lived in Birmingham and Manchester and wrote small-press guides to those cities which the Rough Guide people picked up on and commissioned him to tour Wales, specifically the south and mid, which familiarisation with and consequent admiration of led him to move here permanently in 2000. His social life was hectic, gathering around outdoor parties and their aftermaths, which could last for weeks (I know it). He met a lot of gay people based around Aberystwyth, one of whom called it 'the gay capital of the country', so he used that in the *Rough Guide*. But that said, in the early 1990s there was a gayness in the air that was unusual for a small Welsh seaside town. I like that notion of a free-floating gayness; that it's infectious, that at any moment you might drop your rugby ball and start admiring window displays. 'There is a strain,' Mike says, 'of non-heterosexuality in Welsh culture', and he tells me that many hardcore Welsh nationalists are gay (there's a thread of homophobia in the same culture, too, so it's best not to mention names); indeed, Giraldus Cambrensis wrote: 'It was because of their sins, and more particularly the wicked and detestable vice of homosexuality, that the Welsh were punished by God and so lost first Troy and then Britain', which is an unusual justification for colonialism, if nothing else (and it is nothing else).

Mike wanted to escape the urban, so he first moved to Llangyfelyn, a hamlet between Borth and Tre'r-ddol. Back in Birmingham, only a handful of close friends understood his decision, but 'as a writer', he says, he 'knew this would be the right environment', and again I know what he means. 'There was a culture and passion for art and life in Aber that I couldn't find in the Midlands. And I looked for it'. He was single at the time, and people told him he'd be lynched: 'A gobby English puff would, in mid Wales, be hung from a tree within minutes'. Yet he found a gay community in Tre'r-ddol, neither of whom had ever, not once, been lynched.

After about eighteen months, he moved to Ceinws. His grandmother died[30] and left him enough money for a deposit on a house. Since that move, his relationship to Wales and Welshness has changed 'unrecognisably'; a decade ago, as a guidebook writer, he would see the country as 'a big picture postcard'; that is, his response to it was mainly aesthetic. Now, though, it's 'much more complicated, difficult, and heartbreaking', which he's partly glad of, because it's more true, and partly not happy about, 'because who wouldn't want things to be easier?' The village of Ceinws lies in a landscape 'where things have been ripped out of it or imposed upon it'; like much of Wales, it's a landscape made marginal. Mike's just finished work on the eighth edition of the *Rough Guide*, but he won't do another one; he doesn't feel capable of continuing that breezy tone in regards to his adopted country anymore. Working on the guides has made him hate tourism 'as when it's the only economic hope it's just wrong'.

Beneath Aber's surface, Mike says, 'a lot of strangeness goes on'. He sees the university as 'way too big', sees intolerance creeping into the town as it becomes more homogenised, the high street[31] more uniform and interchangeable with anywhere else. There was a radical political edge to the town in the 1990s that is vanishing, but the town's 'queer heart' will never allow it to be completely swamped by the creeping country-wide banalisation, maybe because, given the emptiness around it, Aber is a metropolis, in relative terms. Its anarchic centre attracts those who live apart from the mainstream; gays, drug users, writers, artists, musicians, etc. 'In the mid 90s there was a nucleus of very Welsh, very puffy, powerful people who have since gone on to hold high positions in Sgrin and S4C,' Mike tells me. 'They're all out now. But still best not to mention names'.

Indeed. Aber's gay landmarks? Well, there was the Boar's Head (often Bowdlerised to the Whore's Bed, where we've already been), The Fountain in Trefechan on a Tuesday night... but the physical gay scene, like many undercultures, has died out all over the place due to the internet; in all towns and cities sex of whatever sort can now be found with a few clicks of a mouse, if you know where in cyberspace to look, so traditional gay haunts in Aber as much as anywhere else 'are disappearing like snow in the sun'. But Aber was never sectarian anyway; 'in most small towns there's one gay pub and you don't be gay anywhere else. But it was always different here'.

Celtic win 2 – 1.

And remember Michael Carson, who you met briefly at Devil's Bridge? Author of *Stripping Penguins Bare* (which I heartily recommend)? Well, he was here, and queer, in the 1960s, when he came down from Liverpool as Michael Wherly, Catholic, 'on the lookout for Dearest Him'[32], who was maybe hiding in the Overseas Students Society in Pantycelyn Hostel. He remembers being baffled by the demonstrations that sought to establish a Welsh-language hall of residence: 'should not university open [the Welsh students] up to the great world, rather than wrap them in their little one?... I would have

gone daft if I had been in a totally English environment at university'
– fair point – 'but I suppose the English are not a group under threat'
– even fairer.

Michael returned to the town in 2000 on a house-hunting mission.
Unlike his namesake, he was unsuccessful, but his visit reminded him
of why he feels an abiding fondness for the place: 'It is off on its own,
surrounded by sea and mountain. Someone reviewing *Stripping* said
Aber was the last refuge of the unambitious male' – remember Herb
Williams? - 'but the same has been said of San Francisco'. He never
would've left in the first place but 'Prince Charles was going [and] I
did not want to share the place with him. Don't know why. Just didn't
fancy it'. He writes that he 'was very "out"' at Aber, 'though not with
the Overseas Students whom, I felt, should be spared such details....
Aberystwyth established an ache in me to travel, to meet people very
different from myself. I did this in country after country, teaching
English. I doubt I'd have grown so much had I gone to Christ's
College'.

So there you go. War machines always benefit from a sprinkle of
gaiety, in my opinion. And I like the ways in which the castle – the
coloniser's great weapon and symbol – has itself been re-colonised; by
lone readers, lovers, children running mad, buskers, the homeless,
sunken-eyed people coming down of a Sunday morning. I've been
there myself, at 9 a.m., sitting whispering on the battlements, staring
out to sea, waiting for the Spar to open so I can buy another bottle of
wine. Not any more, though; the Spar on Terrace Road is now open
24 hours. How the stones echo.

WATER: THE YSTWYTH

The peaks of Pumlumon bubble with springs. One, as we have seen, is
the source of the Rheidol; another, a mere trickle, is the first drip of the
mighty Severn; and only a few miles from that is the first spurt of the
Ystwyth. Light a cigarette sitting next to it and you can tick off all four
elements, that is if one of them doesn't blow or douse another out.

In Welsh, the word 'ystwyth' means 'winding', or 'flexible, pliant,
supple'. John Green, in his book *Afon Ystwyth: The Story of a River*,
points out that the waterway's importance lies not in its contribution
to human trade or traffic but in the ways that it has shaped the
landscape; that it has a magical, not mercantile, significance. Like all
rivers, its course would once have been traced by human movement,

by those seeking the sea or the interior of the country, beneficent as it was with food and water. Permanent settlements would've been made along its banks, at particularly fertile spots. The Ystwyth is only fifteen miles long, yet it gives the name to the town that you're reading about.

Here's the source, at around 1,100 feet up in the Elan Valley (the Pumlumon massif is, well, massive). From the rocks of Esgair Ychion on Bryn Du comes a trickle of extremely clear water. Taste it; it leaves a sweetness on the tongue. It becomes a thicker trickle for a short stretch called the Afon Diliw and then is joined by a second stream behind Craig y Lluest and then descends steeply onto the valley floor where it becomes the Ystwyth. As if the names matter; as if the river would stop its gush and tumble if we'd never named it. Ridge of the Oxen on the Black Hill to the Deluge behind the Rock of the Bothy, the names in English are still gossamer (but quite mellifluous, in the Welsh). Ancient rocks, Silurian and Ordovician, 500 million years old. Moorland. Squeal of a buzzard and of course the trilling river. Cwmystwyth the first village to be found, deep in the valley bottom, still occupied but largely a scattered collection of derelict stone cottages and disused mine workings stippling the steep slopes that reach up to moonscape, the gouged grey rock, the scree, the arrested avalanches of spoil. Morraine: huge boulders around which the river twists. A fault line here which scores the entire valley. Ravens. Is it summer? Well then, the valley walls in parts are thick with heather and gorse, a lilac sheeting, little yellow starbursts releasing vanilla and coconut into the thick fumey air. Is it winter? In that case, all is blasted. Grey and dull brown. Cracks of black in the chasms of ice-rent rocks. Slashes of snow. Heightened water acidity from the conifer plantations doesn't help.

Next, Pontrhydygroes. Built on a bend, one of the Ystwyth's many elbows. The river gets deep and quick here but you can find wee beaches by eddies and peer in; stickleback and caddis fly, boatmen and beetles. Dippers, goosanders. Trout and even salmon, although their return is a slow one. John Green talks about the wonderfully-named polypody ferns that sprout, here, from the oxters of trees and the peregrine eyrie up on the north side of the gorge just past the village. Awesome birds.

Brynafan next. More mining scars on the valley walls. The B4340 crosses the river here between fir and beech and oak and larch and then there's Llanafan and Wenallt and Trawscoed where the river speeds up, spurred by the flatter terrain. The mansion at Trawscoed, now converted into flats, was built by the Vaughan family in 1684. Tyrannical people, by all accounts. John Green quotes the geneticist Professor Steve Jones, who was born on the banks of the Ystwyth, on the Vaughan family: 'classic grinders of the faces of the poor'. One legend goes that, if they wanted rid of a tenant who was exercising his/her rights and refusing to leave, they'd drop a sheep down the chimney, raid the house, accuse the tenant of rustling, and see him/her hanged. Fine people.

Then Llanilar, where, in poor imitation, the river is shadowed by a disused railway line. A good pub here – The Falcon. The line used to link Aberystwyth with Tregaron, before Beeching got his axe out. Still, the hardcore put down beneath the sleepers provides a relatively even riparian walk, through a long and low aviary; the abundance of insects attracts blackcaps and warblers and finches and tits. They whirr and chirrup through the shrubs.

After Llanilar, the river reaches Nanteos, where we won't go again, except to say that a small stream, Nant Paith[33], joins the Ystwyth here and pushes it into Rhydyfelin, beyond which it skirts Pen Dinas and reaches, as it's always longed to do, the sea. Float out on it. Sooner or later the tide will bring you back in again.

HARBOUR

I like the harbour. Swans. A grebe, once, great-crested, swimming peeping and lost between the pleasure boats, some of which are bigger than my house. The posh flats – mostly holiday homes – look out over it all, part of the ongoing plan to do an Eliza Doolittle on the area, the same plan that's been implemented in every sizeable seaside town and city across the British Isles, and which, in every case, will never entirely succeed, because harbours remember their mud. These places where humans put themselves to sea, they'll never be completely gentrified and prettified because they've seen the yearning in the human soul which always leaves wreckage, of some shape or form.

The surface might gleam, but peer beneath. Malcolm Pryce, in an email, wrote: 'Down by the harbour, people no longer fish, they surf. In wetsuits! The surfers are very good, but I can't help feeling it's a bit unseemly'. People do still fish here, of course, but I take his point (and love that 'unseemly'). And Matt Jarvis's fine but, at the time of writing, unpublished long poem 'An Aberystwyth Canto' begins:

at the harbour, I said, so we went and looked and we tried to take
      it all in
with apartments and a marina
the pleasure-boats at rest
when she shook her head at an angry thought...
I stand on the sea-wall as the waves track in, watching the surfers
      catch the
            rip
that sandbank, he said with a grunt, it's always been a problem
and the cars along the promenade
I look at you as you shade your eyes

Harbours are neither really land nor water, so they seem to attract the desire to make something figuratively final or solid. They're familiar with one of the darknesses in our hearts. Five years ago, here, a death-obsessed young boy persuaded his girlfriend to commit suicide. Or attempted to; she fell off the jetty onto rocks, suffered serious head injuries, but happily she's alive, as are, indeed, all parties involved, very much so, which forestalls any further discussion of the matter. But no amount of cosmetic work or prohibitively expensive moorings or rocketing house prices will ever stop boats from leaving here every day to dredge up and fetch from the slime far below things profoundly offensive to human sense. And, of course, the ingredients for a nice bouillabaisse.

The town's constable, in 1280, pressed for the building of a harbour to signal and spur the new settlement's prosperity. The estuary where the two piers join each other and the sea was the obvious place to site it. Wharves and jetties were built on the spot; wooden, and therefore weak. Storms caused much damage, as they still do, as did the harbour bar, to shipping. The bar wasn't lowered until the long stone jetty was built in 1836.

See the signs of vanished industry; the conical malt-drying kiln on the Trefechan side of the harbour, for one. Shipbuilding is no more, but it was once huge; in tye century between 1778 and 1880 nearly 300 sailing ships were built here, from thirty-ton sloops to galleons of more than ten times the size, with the secondary industries of sail-making and the manufacture of chains and anchors etc. The ships stopped appearing in the late 1800s but boatbuilding went on until 1959 at Williams's yard in Trefechan, which specialised in lifeboats during World War Two. Attempts were once made to connect Aberystwyth by steamship with Liverpool and Bristol, but the advent of the railway line rendered this unnecessary; nice, but unnecessary.

Fish, of course, have always propped up the harbour; once it was herring, now it's mackerel and bass and crabs and lobsters (it's always puzzled me, the modern British aversion to herring). Lead ore was the principal export into the early years of the last century; St. David's Wharf, beneath Pen Dinas where the harbour narrows, was used for this purpose and was connected to the Aber-Carmarthen railway line. Grain was exported too; dairy produce; even people, most famously on the brigs *Credo* and *Anne Jenkins*, mainly to North America and Canada. Now people enter the harbour to berth, not board, boats; the marina, built in 1994, can accommodate 103 vessels. And some of them are huge, as I've said; I'd get lost on them. So if the harbour now is an *entrepôt*, then it distributes only privilege (which isn't entirely fair, I know, but...).

On October 5th, 1745, forty-seven boats caught around a million and a half fish, worth £1,400, in one night. Impossible, now, in British seas, but the harbour waters do teem, largely with pollock and mullet that can grow to huge sizes, scaly torpedoes nosing beneath the keels. Mullet are notoriously bad to eat, but I once slow-roasted a watermelon-sized portion of one over a beach fire and it was utterly delicious (but, then again, I was very, very hungry). The harbour also provides 'casual' – meaning 'backbreaking' – work on the dredgers; boring and heavy labour, but long hours can be had and thus a lot of money made.

Another point of note; the civil engineer employed in 1834 to improve the harbour, and who suggested the construction of the stone pier, was a Mr. George Bush. No relation, I hope.

BRIDGE STREET/MAES IAGO/PIER STREET

Bridge Street is frozen; it is the centre of development, and indeed a link between changed Trefechan and the top of the town with its new bars and take-aways appearing every year, but the street itself has less been changed by recent building work or development of euphemistic amenity than any other in the town. Start at the town side of Trefechan Bridge and go up. Divert into Powell Street and have a look at the Tabernacl and Rutelli's war memorial in the forecourt. The Tabernacl, in the late 1700s and early 1800s, was a focal meeting-house for Calvinist Methodists. When it was built, this area was devoid of dwellings, but it's now a cross-hatching of terraces and ginnels, tightly-packed. The back of Y Tabernacl, facing Mill Street, is bland and foursquare, and the (at the time of writing) current graffiti campaign which has adorned it with stencilled staring eyes has made it a lot more interesting, but the front of it, on Powell Street, is architecturally striking. As is the interior of St. Mary's Church on Gray's Inn Road, another Bridge Street capillary. Begun in 1865 to a design of William Butterfield's on land donated by Colonel Powell of Nanteos (aw Jeez, him again), the foundation stone was laid on the 27th April by Miss Morice of Carrog. The corbels that carry the roof are worth a gander. Miss Morice hailed from Carrog House on Bridge Street, which now houses the RAFA Club, and was the home of the Reverend Thomas

Richards, friend of Wilberforce and John Keble, and not the only noteworthy personage to have lived on Bridge Street. Anthony Brockway, webmaster of the 'wolfman knew my father' site (Google it) and knowledgeable fount of many things Welsh and odd, tells me about David Ivan Jones, a famous Communist who lived here, and who went to South Africa in search of a cure for his TB and became one of the first whites to champion equal rights for black South Africans, was imprisoned and is still honoured by the African National Congress and the SA Communist Party. He later went to live in the USSR where he became an associate and translator of Lenin (and has, I hope, paid for these sins in purgatory). Moscow gave him a full state funeral. Gwyn A. Williams co-authored a book about him, but I've been unable to track this down.

Then there's Dr. Ric Williams, a physician, who established the Marine Baths in 1799. The Ship Bank used to occupy No. 43, and was perhaps the oldest bank in Wales; the Black Sheep Bank could be found here too, so-called because its £1 note had a black sheep on it and its £2 note, unsurprisingly, two. Powerful local squires had townhouses up here; the Pughs of Abermad and the Pryses of Gogerddan. This is where they'd strut and cavort and lend their presence to this once most important thoroughfare. Sir Hugh Myddelton lived here in the 1630s, he of the New River Scheme which supplied clean water to London from the Ware (and amassed a vast fortune from his mining enterprises hereabouts).

Yr Hen Llew Du, the Old Black Lion, is one of only two surviving pubs on the street, from around 1700. It's loud and lively of an evening and a pleasant place to while away some hours of an afternoon, especially during the winter in the snug, warmed by a log fire. It once housed the Princess of Wales mail coach which ran twice a week to Shrewsbury and back and the cobbled pavement anterior to it is a pre-macadam remnant. Other bars have appeared in this street in recent years, but they don't last long; the Llew, and the Nag's Head opposite, are pub enough for one street. Tiffany Atkinson, university lecturer and resident poet, has a piece in her latest collection[34] called 'Black Lion Prophet', which perfectly evokes one atmospheric aspect of this fine hostelry:

> He's drunk of course   though not in the modern
> way   His style's more oldee testament   Old

nicotine-fingered Moses   picking splinters
of psalm from his teeth   Which isn't to say
he's a nice bloke   or an easy or polite bloke
only   fuck la politesse   he's   well he's
good   a grand old cunt   like Gandhi say
or   Winston Churchill even   And the thing
is   is he'll turn what you say on a sixpence
till you don't know head from tail   then slide
his own thoughts in on the backdraft   and
when you're this close to decking him
he does this blessing thing   dead casual   like
he's frisking a fly from your forehead   or
finessing a string quartet through a soft
parabola of Mozart   and he does it   and
you feel your inner contours   sure as whiskey
on a morning-after gut   but deeper   and for one
outrageous moment you could stitch a life
from off-cuts fringed with glory   And that's
how he rakes over your heart's old cockle-bed
or something like it   How he dredges up
and glams such rag-and-bone antiques as
goodness   evil   grace   forgiveness   and
that old fang in the ankle   sod it   love

Lines twenty two and twenty three here have a peculiar echo; on
the Bridge Street/Gray's Inn Road corner is the old town-house for
the great Gogerddan family, built on the site of the First House of
Correction, where the miscreant or workshy (and, probably, the
simply shy) were made to work a treadmill. Excavations here have
unearthed many human bones – those worked to death or afflicted
with untreated injury or disease. I wonder if the Gogerddan family
ever had their sleep disturbed, in that house, by wailing or weeping.

Take another quick detour, down Queen Street. A crumbling brick
wall about halfway down bears the graffiti 'COFIWCH ABERTH
ABERGELE', or 'Remember the Martyrs of Abergele'. These are
Alwyn Jones and George Taylor who, on the night of June 30th 1969,
accidentally blew themselves up. Alwyn was twenty-two, George
thirty-seven, both married, and with young children. Prince Charles
was on his way to Caernarfon castle to be granted the title of Prince
of Wales, a symbolic act of colonial administration quite extraordinary in a modern western democracy. George and Alwyn weren't

going to let this happen; they were going to plant a bomb that would derail the prince's train. But as they were assembling the device in a passageway between government offices in Abergele, it went off; Alwyn was blown forty yards. 'Both corpses,' Roy Clews wrote[35], 'were a bloodily mutilated, unrecognisable wreckage of bone and tissues'. North Wales filled up with Special Branch; Charles got

himself invested. A commemorative parade passes through Abergele every year on June 30th. Every movement needs its martyrs. Charlie himself might've been one, had the bomb-plot worked; and had it worked, I'm sure modern Welsh militancy would have many more than two.

Back on Bridge Street, turn left onto Princes Street. Go past Ystwyth Books, a superb shop, both brand new and second hand, and always likely to offer up a gem. On the corner of Custom House Street stands the Ship and Castle, one of the oldest pubs in the town, host to a number of real ales and live music sessions. Further down this street is a thin alleyway that leads to a mews courtyard in which a chalybeate well can be seen. The word 'chalybeate' comes from the modern Latin chalybeatus, which in turn comes from the Greek khalups, meaning 'steel', and refers to natural mineral springs that contain iron salts. There were other such wells in Aberystwyth; one was sunk in land adjacent to Alexandra Road that became a railway goods yard. The health-giving properties of the water drawn from it was, as is typical with such things, very much exaggerated.

Bridge Street terminates at Maes Iago, or St. James's Square. Clwb Yoko is here, one of the town's nightspots, and the Dolphin, an excellent chippy, and other take-aways and shops and chapel-become-pub Yr Academi. Here, too, is the town clock, on the site of the old town hall; the original structure went up in 1856 and stood sixty two feet high and cost £1,250 to build. It had a spiral staircase with a small viewing gallery at the top but was demolished in 1956 and replaced by another one which was in turn demolished in recent years as it was deemed 'unsafe', although I heard that dynamite was needed to bring it down, so sturdy was it. On Saturday nights, it looks out over pande-monium of that punchy and pukey sort that can be seen in any sizeable town in modern Britain. Best avoided at such times, really. But branching off from it is Pier Street, which, if Aber has a café culture, is it. There's the Penguin Café, famous as the place where the Trefechan Bridge protestors discussed their options in the early 60s, the Cabin with it's monochromatic iconic images of Bogart and Monroe etc., the great tapas restaurant (La Taverna) down the wee side street, the Home Café which doubles as an oriental restaurant after sundown.... Galloways is here too, a superb independent bookshop. As is the adult shop, Nice 'n' Naughty, with its window displays of fluffy handcuffs and saucy costumery. The location, I'll wager, deters some prospective customers; I mean, those of a meddling mind[36] can sit in the big Cabin windows over a pot of tea and check who enters the shop: 'Oo, there's Mr. Jones! That pink PVC catsuit doesn't suit him. Wrong colour, that'. And there's Ultracomida, a wonderful continental deli, full of strange cheese and sausages and wines and olives and cornichons and Welsh beer and bread and all manner of things else. The only place to shop on a summer's day when you're planning on spending the afternoon amongst grass and flowers and bees somewhere. Great sarnies, too.

Pier Street leads down to the pier. What a surprise.

GREAT DARKGATE STREET/
NORTH PARADE/CAMBRIAN STREET

This is the town's aorta. The quintessential and atypical bustling small-town high street with its chainstores (Woolworth's, Superdrug) and banks and caffs. At the top, opposite Maes Iago's clock, where Badlandz surf-shop now stands, note the Georgian facade with the pillared porch; it was once the town's main pub, the Gogerddan Arms, later called the Lion Royal, and then Padarn Hall. Now you can buy a wetsuit in there, should the need or fancy take you. Opposite this, down Market Street, a feng shui shop once stood, but it didn't last long; perhaps it was in the wrong place. You'll find the Orangery down there, an upmarket kind of drinking establishment where you can nibble on a bowl of marinated olives with your special-ist Spanish beer. Very pleasant. It's been several kinds of drinking den over the years, but this one looks like it'll stay, popular as it is.

The Post Office sports a fine mosaic fascia, and the Halifax opposite bears a plaque recording the site of the Great Darkgate, the town's main landward gate which provided an entry through the wall from the east in the medieval period. It was also the town's last House of Correction in 1789, where vagabonds and beggars and other ne'er-do-wells were held and put to work as a rehabilitative measure (its present office can be somewhat punitive in its effects, too). This 'work' amounted, often, to little more than public torture; both male and female 'offenders' were stripped and whipped to ribbons whilst pulling laden carts from here to Trefechan Bridge and back. The House was demolished in 1892 and replaced by a police station.

The HSBC bank, further up[37], stands on a town pound; stray sheep, cattle, horses, pigs and geese were held here until they could be bailed out by their owners. Back in Market Street, the Talbot Hotel (one of those inns which the Orangery has superseded), had a member of staff in the 1780s who was said to be 117 years old and who would shave the braver of the residents after a nip of whiskey or two. This tiny thoroughfare once boasted six taverns, as did Upper Great Darkgate Street, one of which, the Skinner's Arms, had the town stocks.

At the other end of the street, on North Parade, the Upper Limit caff serves what the *Observer* food magazine called 'the best breakfast in Wales'. It is, unarguably, very good. One afternoon a couple of years ago ITV Wales, as part of their Great Welsh Cafés series, filmed in here. The images of people lighting up cigarettes with their mugs of tea already seem like a glimpse into an ancient age, and it's in here that I imagine Saunders Lewis conceiving his poem 'A Scene in a Café'[38] (although of course he leaves the establishment unnamed) with it's Eliotian visions of the living dead: 'The mottled throng/The sad throng that had lost the goodness of understanding', even if the staff and patrons in here tend to be a cheery and pleasant bunch altogether. Another brilliant curmudgeon lived in this area – the inimitable and treasurable Caradoc Evans, who, in October 1944, moved to 36A North Parade from New Cross with his wife Marguerite, and who experienced the heart troubles here that would shortly kill him just a few months later on 11 January 1945. Caradoc's connections with Aberystwyth aren't hawsers. He was born in Rhydlewis and grew up in Llandysul, and so Carmarthen's really his town, but he first moved here from London in 1935, probably to be close to his ailing mother and with aspirations to live by his writing, which he quickly realized he couldn't do and so became the kept man of the well-off Maguerite[39]. He seems to have left Aber at this time under a cloud – his first wife, Rose, sued him for unpaid alimony. He began a novel set in the town – *The Holy City* – but soon abandoned it. His return to the area in 1939 saw him living next door to Saunders Lewis at Abermad; here he wrote *Morgan Bible*, reviewed by Lewis favourably, who remarked on Evans's need to 'refresh' the English language, 'to create from it a personal, new and particular language, before English can be a means of artistic creation'[40]. Oh to have been a dung-fly on a cowpat when those two took their daily constitutionals across the fields.

Professor George H. Green, in his essay 'Caradoc'[41], writes that the novelist didn't belong in Aberystwyth, no more than he belonged in London (which is belied by Caradoc's journal entry that reads 'God never meant me to live in the country'[42]), but he evidently enjoyed some opulence; Green called at his North Parade gaff one day and a maid took his card and showed him into a lavishly decorated dining room to await Caradoc[43]. Even more astonishing, then, the clarity of the depiction of horrendous rural poverty in much of his work, including *Morgan Bible*, in which he utters the wonderful line 'a happy Welshman is as rare as a bee in the snow'. Dylan Thomas and Glyn Jones came to visit Evans in Aber roundabout this time; the story told to them about the eccentric Chartist Dr. William Price, who became responsible for the legitimisation of cremation, shocked Thomas into dropping his cigarette on his hotel bed and burning several holes in the sheets[44].

So Aberystwyth can lay claim to a bit of Caradoc Evans, not entirely unconvincingly. It's incredible, Evans's work. It stinks and seethes with mud and anger. It's magnificent, mouldy stuff. It's not what I'm looking for right now, however, in the Oxfam bookshop next door to the Upper Limit (in which I've just wolfed down a full breakfast and am feeling surprisingly unbloated); rather, I'm looking for Isaac Bashevis Singer. No connection to Aber whatsoever, but I'd received a letter that morning from a reader in America telling me that the only story to have made her cry more than a certain one of my own was Singer's 'A Crown of Feathers' so I'm searching for this funny little Jewish feller who can make distant ladies weep as much as I can and this second-hand bookshop is a good place to look and indeed I do find him, here, between Seiffert and Steinbeck, Penguin *Collected*, three quid. Great stuff. I buy it and head towards the bus stop, following North Parade around into Cambrian Street where I realize I've got an hour or so to wait for the bus so I give Keith Morris a knock. I'd been meaning to anyway.

It's another hot day. Cambrian Street is a quiet retreat in the town, even though the blur of Terrace Road is visible at its end. Keith lives here, opposite the antiques store, in which I once saw the best bed ever, but well out of my affordability range. He's a professional photographer, whose new book of Aber-based work is due out from Gomer in 2008. His Aber roots run very, very deep; his mother was the town mayor twice, once in the 70s and again in the 90s, and his love for the town runs just as deep. He talks about its layers, 'which don't overlap but dovetail' – students, residents, visitors. He calls it 'New York lite' – 'not that it never sleeps but that it has different rhythms throughout the year'. The house he lives in belonged to his grandfather, and he was brought up in Cambrian Street after being born in what is now the car park of Bronglais hospital, when of course it was the maternity ward; 'my active life has been about living in this one street', which is built almost entirely on sandy soil reclaimed from the sea. He remembers the Barn Centre which used to be situated here, as, indeed, do many of the people I speak to; this was a former ironworks which had been part of the university and which housed the drama department, the place where Brith Gof and Arad Goch held their first rehearsals. The space was opened up to other artists at rent so cheap that people could pay it out of their dole money. The building was demolished for flats in 1992, which means that, as Keith says, 'while Aber is now a great place to see art, there's no creative centre here anymore'. Still, the spirit remains, and with that the potential; and anyway, Arad Goch's space on Bath Street is, at the time of writing, undergoing extensive renovation. Keith lived in California between 1984 and 1986 on a Welsh Arts Council grant to photograph ex-pat Cymru over there, who are rapidly disappearing: 'The Irish and Scots and the Italians etc. have percolated into the American consciousness but the Welsh haven't'[45]. He returned to Wales 'due to a sense of unfinished business; unfocused and nebulous, just something I felt I had to do' (again, this is a sentiment I will hear reiterated by those with strong Aber connections). The town is a great place to raise a family, Keith says, and his daughters will stay here, although of course he'd like them to see 'the outside world', which the world does seem to be, in Aberystwyth.

In relation to his work, he's been photographing Aberystwyth for over a quarter of a century and his archive has become a historical document, given the velocity of change that the town's experiencing. 'The 'now' is very quickly becoming the 'then', here', he says: 'Photography is all about mortality'. And perspective, I say....

Aber is an island. It's geographically isolate. It competes with no other town in the vicinity: 'It sails on in a bubble of consciousness with a status bigger than it's physical size. It has no chip on its shoulder; it has nothing to prove. It has the National Library, the university, the Urdd, various publishers.... There's a feeling that there's more happening than one would expect in a town of this size'. Keith mentions a 'cordon sanitaire' around the town, and 'a relaxed west-coast vibe like California.... Being where the sun sets is more relaxing; compare Perth to Brisbane, say[46]. The west encourages mellowness, open-ness, and tolerance[47]'.

Well, maybe. There is, after all, Johnathan Raban's take on the west, that 'solitaries, sociopaths, compulsive travellers, boys who had failed to grow up found their way inevitably west, where they could pass for normal citizens. Fear of long-term attachment, to any thing or any body, was not a disability out here'[48]. The ships don't sail anymore but the world reaches out to itself nevertheless. I like talking to Keith.

At home, I sit down with Singer and turn to 'A Crown of Feathers'. The phone rings. That was almost a year ago and I still haven't read the story.

WATER: THE SEA

Even at the inland rim of the town you can sometimes hear it. Even several miles inland – at the top of Pendam, say – you can sometimes smell it, if the wind's blowing in the right direction. The town is built on it, figuratively on its bounty and literally on its morraine. It entices. Throws up surprising things. A carpet of starfish, hundreds of thousands of them, turning the entire sweep of the beach orange for a day. Corpses of seals. A huge deepwater buoy. Cetaceans can be seen, the smaller species, a glimpse of fin and gleaming back in the waves.

In 1826, on one summer morning, a farmer went down to the edge of his littoral field to gaze at the ocean, as people do. There he saw an attractive young woman sporting in the waves. After a good, long look he went to fetch his family and they concealed themselves to gawp, but the wife, annoyed at this voyeurism, strode onto the beach and shouted and the young woman swam away, revealing a large scaly tail. Interestingly, the family's report scarcely mentions the tail, focusing instead on the 'handsome' face and 'blameless' breast and the only sound she made, 'a noise like sneezing'[49].

Gwyneth Lewis, Wales's first national poet and the author of the

best five-word poem in English[50], isn't from Aberystwyth but she too
feels its pull. Her first acquaintance with the town was due to car-
sickness as a child (like me), and she often returns. She has remarked,
suitably poetically, on the view from in front of the public shelter on
the promenade, 'one of the most aesthetically pleasing places in all
Wales'[51], with the repeated horizontals in the lines of the zebra cross-
ing and the kerbstones and the bars of the railings and then the
horizon itself, 'like lines of poetry', she says, even though the view's
been marred by the verticals of the flagpoles to fly Butler's banners.
'I'm appalled,' she told me recently; 'Aber is going so upmarket. Its
mixture of the prissy and the promiscuous is what makes it so deeply
human'. She was here to witness the beached buoy, and with her
permission, I'll quote the poem she wrote about it in its entirety[52]. It's
called 'The Buoy':

> As soon as it arrived, the buoy
> became a talking point
> and, therefore, a landmark
> or, should I say, a sea-
>
> mark, as the latest storm
> had dragged it adrift
> from the Milford shipping lanes,
> dumped it in Aber. It exerted charm
>
> far from the place it was meant to be
> as a guide to traffic,
> though walkers still came
> to discuss it solemnly where it lay
>
> tied on the beach like a thirty-foot pet,
> held by two anchors.
> It drew out all the usual in us:
> someone tried to force open the plate
>
> that protected the radar
> equipment inside, but the bolts
> were welded so fast
> against vandals and water

that both were defeated. Along its frame
writing sprouted in limpet words -
Dan x 3, POLI, LOVE
I woz ere – all looking for fame

on a foreign body. Strange,
how words keep on meaning
though we don't always mean
their knowing. It was out of range

of all receivers that could understand
the gen it transmitted –
when not on its side,
a heavy floater, stuck in the sand

and yet it kept telling about its fate
in the sea's horizons,
how iron can float
by virtue of vacuum inside.

It defied description. Lunar module?
Shuttlecock? But it showed
the strength of water
by its standing still,

a mote of dust that proved the light,
a Jesus object, an impediment
that reveals the impossible to grasp.
Its ferris wheel became a famous sight

so people took photos while the sea
crackled like electricity
around their sneakers.
Me, I lay in a B & B

further along the pebbly prom.
The Funkin Pussy Posse
played U.S. House all night. Drunks
swore like radar on their way home.

> I lay like a planet, one side of my face
> lit up by belisha beacon moons
> every three seconds.
> You'll never fathom the wit of grace.

There's a call and a pull to the sea that dominates great port cities, let alone small towns. Our amphibian brains and whatever internal organs evolved out of our swim bladders cannot help but respond. Not as if it's safe, that cold and hunted place. Not as if it's refuge, although maybe the promise of pre-birth recall suggests so. An escape from gravity. Freedom from that thudding through the soles which takes up metronomic monotony in the skull.

Or simply possibility, the damply palpable highway to other lands, the thought of which so delighted us as children. Evan Yardley, the adventurer and mystery-man touched by espionage who settled in Aberystwyth, wrote in his autobiographical novel *Five o'Clock Shadows* about how a young man vacillating between joining the army or navy need only walk past Aberystwyth pier and up onto Penparcau to look out across Cardigan Bay to Ireland and the Atlantic beyond to make up his mind and go Jacktar-wards[53].

Aberystwyth's inseparable from its waters, both brine and brackish. The town's strata, the fluidity of it's history and cultural identity, is mirrored in each exulting boom, each susurrant soft collapse, each disapproving hiss.

RAILWAY STATION

Arriva Trains Wales, the only rail company to serve mid-Wales after privatisation, has improved its services of late; now, only one in three trains is tardy, they're not overheated, there's usually a trolley service, there is soap and water in the toilets and a blessed absence of overflowing ordure, the carriages are comparatively clean, and with the addition of two extra carriages on busy services, passengers aren't sardined anymore. Privatisation is fine in principle, but in the absence of competition, that principle doesn't hold. It's ridiculous. The first leg of a rail journey to London was becoming so unpleasant that people were opting to take the bus to Carmarthen and travelling on from there. Why pay a fortune for cramped conditions and missed connections in an overheated and smelly cattle truck? Recent small improvements have been very welcome. But bus is still better. I've travelled by rail in so-called 'developing' countries and the service has been immeasurably more reliable and comfortable than it is, or has been up until very recently, between Aberystwyth and Birmingham. Lot cheaper, too.

Anyway. The station was opened on June 23rd 1864, when Cambrian Railways linked the town with Whitchurch and Shrewsbury, and in 1867 the Manchester and Milford Railway arrived, providing a link with south Wales via Carmarthen (which line was scrapped by Beeching in 1964). Great Western Railways took over both companies in 1922 and two years later built the station building, the neo-classical main block with the clock tower. The original glass canopy still remains, netted now to prevent pigeons roosting in the rafters and crapping into the provender of Wetherspoon's customers below (the pub chain bought and occupied the station building a few years ago). It's a great place to watch an electric storm. Craft occupies part of the building adjacent to the pub; it's a non-profit company that re-cycles furniture, books, clothes, bikes etc. and sells them on cheaply, and as such it's a valuable and important place. The promotional bumf advertises 'everything from a tea-spoon to a three-piece-suite', and it's not exaggerating. There's also a collection service; Craft will send a man in a van to take away your unwanted furniture. The pub pew I'm sitting on as I write this in my kitchen was bought from there. Dead cheap.

The narrator of Gwyneth Lewis's poem 'Welsh Espionage' alights at this train station and asks for directions: 'Ticket collector quizzed me: Did I know/ the pubs or the chapels better?' [54]. This is a real-life enquiry; it was asked of Gwyneth herself. Typically Aberystwyth, that pubs or chapels are taken as landmarks, as places to get one's bearings from. It was the desire to promote the town as the 'Brighton of Wales' that prompted the advent of the railway line, enthusiastically and, by all accounts persuasively, propounded by a G.H. Whalley in the very early 1860s to the then mayor, Robert Edwards. Work on the line began in 1862 and by autumn the line lay within two miles of Borth but storms (and maybe the *gwrach y cors*) made the drive across the bog extremely difficult and the navvies rebelled; police were called in to quash disturbances. The first train to arrive at Borth was twenty-three carriages long and brought in 600 people from Oswestry, Shrewsbury and Welshpool at 2s.6d. a head. Apparently the day was so hot that many of the passengers stripped naked and ran into the sea. On the day the track reached Aberystwyth, guns were fired throughout the day, flags and banners flew, and all the

ships in the harbour, despite
the death of their trade that the
railway heralded, were rigged
out with the whole range of
colour-codes and signals. The
first train arrived at noon,
thirty-five coaches long and
carrying 1,800 passengers.
That night, at the Belle Vue
Hotel, the dinner for the
'notables' was vast; W.J. Lewis,
in *Born on a Perilous Rock*, lists
the entire menu. I count fifty
two items, including turtle

soup, 'compote of pigeons', 'Calves head a la Tortue', 'raised pies',
'aspic of prawns' and 'lobster cheese' (the belly boggles). The feast-
ers didn't want to leave. The return train reached Oswestry at 3 a.m.

The Vale of Rheidol terminus shares the same concourse with the
main branch line. The Manchester and Milford railway company had
been given permission to use this route to achieve their aim of
rivalling Liverpool as the main import of American cotton (you see?
Envy and resentment from Manchester even then towards the well-
hung docker fifty miles to the west). Nothing came of the plan, so the
route was left fallow until talks resumed concerning a narrow-gauge
link to Devil's Bridge and work began on that line in 1901. Labour
was difficult to find until the Elan valley reservoirs were completed
and hundreds of Irish navvies found themselves unoccupied. The line
opened in 1902 and saw a boom period during the hysterical and
countrywide religious revival of 1904-06, when preaching meetings
were held in the Rheidol valley at isolated chapels and churches now
rendered reachable. The closure of the lead mines forced the line into
desuetude just before the First World War, although it's never
completely closed due to the tourist trade, even if British Rail has
stripped the line of much that was of historical value. It now runs
from Aberystwyth to Devil's Bridge between March and October,
through some pretty spectacular scenery, at one point climbing 600
feet. It's not cheap to travel on it, but it's worth it, at least once, and
for a two quid supplement you can travel first class, although what
that involves over and above the standard class service I don't know.

So the railway line still ensures that, in the summer months, Aber
becomes a West Country suburb. I wonder if the townsfolk of the

1860s had their own equivalent of one of the most popular fine-weather jokes to be heard across Cardigan Bay: What's the difference between a Brummie and an Easyjet? The plane stops whining when it lands at Alicante (don't shoot the messenger, my Brummagem buddies).

MILL STREET, ALEXANDRA ROAD AND CAPILLARIES

If Great Darkgate Street is the town's aorta, this is the vena cava; it stretches from the start of Trefechan Bridge to the edge of the Buarth and allows traffic – which often backs up from here to the top of Penglais Hill – to skirt the town as part of the one-way system onto the A487, or ferries it down the Boulevard St. Brieuc (named after one of Aber's twin towns) into Llanbadarn. It's perpetually busy; there's the traffic avoiding the town centre, pick-ups and drop-offs at the railway station, shoppers for the retail park, taxis pulling into and out of the rank and the bus stops for non-local services – Cardiff and Bangor and all stops in between. London, too. There's several pubs – the Mill, the Lord Beechings, the Vale of Rheidol, a twenty-four-hour garage, and a small, independent (and very good) record shop in Backbeat Records. A bookies, too. And some place that's got something to do with mobile phones.

Mill Street is named after Our Lady's Mill, built around 1280 to grind the district's corn. In 1530 it was decreed that profits from that should pay for religious services at the newly built St. Mary's church (which collapsed into the sea, remember?); if anybody objected to this, it's not on record. The leat that fed the waterwheels ran along the sides of the road, and both leat and wheel are long gone, but some of the mill still stands. At the roundabout is the Salvation Army Hall, built in 1844 as an English Wesleyan Chapel. Opposite that is the former Board School, opened in 1874, still operating as a school.

It's just a thoroughfare, a bit run-down (indeed, it prompted a relative visiting from Australia to remark that parts of the town were a 'shithole', but forgive him; he's a naturalized Aussie), with the terraced houses not given over to students absurdly overpriced[55]. It caters for little more than traffic, really, and most amenities – garage, roundabout etc. - are commensurate with that. The capillaries are of greater interest, particularly Chalybeate Street; the *Cambrian News* of May 4th 2006 printed a remarkable letter written a century earlier which bewailed the amount of entrails clogging up the street at the time: 'May I be allowed to express... my disgust and astonishment at the disregard of some of our tradespeople for the health of the town generally. Take Chalybeate Street as an instance... wading through a collection of the entrails and skins of sheep and other animals, the whole soaking in pools of blood.... Now, sir, you will agree with me that in a

town aspiring to be a health resort, this is a deplorable state of things. The practice of throwing dead and decaying fish and animal matter about the streets and sidewalks is indescribably filthy, and the people responsible ought to be dealt with by the local governing authority'.

Ooer. There's no such scenes today to prod into apoplexy that Edwardian gentleman; the only butcher present is spotlessly clean and the rabbits and pheasants sometimes strung up from the awnings outside have been previously bled. There's a grocer's opposite, and a large hardware store. Mecca coffee house. Healthfood emporium. Florists. Never any blood to be seen, not even at the weekends, given the absence of drinking establishments and take-aways here (although Corners restaurant will supply a good bottle of wine), but I did once witness the squashing of a pigeon beneath the wheels of a post-van pulling out of the main sorting office car park. I saw some entrails then, by God. Not very many of them, but I still wish I hadn't. Ick.

PEN DINAS AND CONSTITUTION HILL: MONUMENT, FUNICULAR, AND CAMERA OBSCURA

Pen Dinas and Constitution Hill are like two great green gateposts, doorjambs, framing the town between them. They stand in direct physical opposition to each other; stand on top of one and you can see the top of the other, the town spread below, unless a low grey cloud or hanging sheet of poised drizzle obscures the view, as it often does. When I lived at the foot of Constitution Hill I'd often climb it as bad weather blew in from Ireland. I'd take a flask of tea under the awning

of the old rickety caff up there and watch the squalls approach like immense grey ghosts over the sea.

A fair bit of renovation work has gone on at the top of Consti in recent times. The rickety funicular still shuttles the idle or infirm or curious to the top, but the old caff has been superseded by a much swankier establishment. There's a tremendous view from up here. Paul Henry – who you've already met – had a summer job on the Cliff Railway when he was a boy, 'sometimes outside' he told me in an email, 'near the cliff-edge, burning litter passengers had dropped.... Only one-legged, elderly Ted was allowed to drive the trams, which were operated from a control room at the top of the steep line. This meant that the first ride every day was dependent on Ted having installed himself in his nest'. In the same email, Paul continues: 'Picture Ted, then, circa 1972 (before the national obsession with Health and Safety at work had kicked in), pendulous Ted, in a bus-conductor's cap, each morning negotiating the zig-zag path to the top of Consti.... He moved at a pace, higher... higher still... swinging his boot, somewhere between a fable and a Monty Python sketch. But heroic all the same. He was saving the town, wasn't he? Ascending on wooden wings, out of the early sun, the red Danger sign at the foot of the path, and all so that "able-bodied" sloths could be hauled by his cable up the same hill.... Maybe they should pull down Victory from her column by the castle and replace her with Ted. One stony crutch could be raised northward, victoriously, in the direction of Constitution Hill'.

Beautiful stuff. Trust a poet. On a clear day the view from the summit extends from the Llyn peninsula in the north to Strumble Head in the south, while inland Snowdon, Cadair Idris, Pumlumon and the Preselis can be seen. That's a vista of over 1,000 square miles, over 100 miles of coastline and twenty six mountain peaks, and indeed the act of seeing is what this hill is all about; the old caff is now being used to house exhibitions of visual art, the first by Rooth Calvert-Ennals, locally-based, called *Songs of Seaside Lives*, in mixed media. And Pictiwrs ar Daith, a new film society, had the inspired idea of screening Hitchcock's *Vertigo* up here (as well as Jaws on the beach, and *Casablanca* in the Casablanca restaurant). Plus, of course, there's the camera obscura; train it on the town and see how many friends and acquaintances you can spot; which ones look furtive, which ones look like they've already taken a drink. Follow them from bank to bookies to boozer. A great way to spy.

The top of Consti was once called Luna Park – a large amusement area. There was a restaurant, a pavilion, a bandstand, gardens, terraces, an open-air dance floor, an earlier camera obscura, several kiosks, a small scenic railway, and several covered seating areas. Japanese lanterns lit it up at night-time and there were frequent firework displays, but the location's exposed nature, and the attendant gales and rains, forced it to close. But even just sitting up here is pleasant enough, except for those who choose this spot to attempt suicide or fall foul of drunken misadventure. It is high. The sea-cliffs are sheer. Large braziers, on significant dates, burn signal fires, visible for many miles. Impressive, if a bit Wicker Man-ish. Climbing the steep and zig-zag path one midnight my heart almost burst as a barn owl rose up from the grass before me; face to face, mere inches apart, hovering spectre, luminous white. The bird seemed less startled than I.

A traverse rope could be slung between the peaks of Consti and Pen Dinas, so closely do they mirror each other, but I wouldn't use it because that would be paralysingly terrifying – much nicer to have a stroll through the town to Consti's twin overlooking Tan y Bwlch, the 'gap of fire', the south beach. This hill sports no attractions other than the monument and the view. And the silence; all town-sounds have vanished, up here, and people, especially on a weekday, rarely visit. There's a bit of a breeze, some cropping sheep, and the chirruping of little birds and the whirring of their wings.

Pen Dinas is basically a hill-fort, dating from about 600 B.C. (there was an even older settlement below it, on the narrow coastal plain). It's well fortified; the earthworks are still clearly visible and excavations, which still periodically take place, have revealed sunken hut circles on which

round, thatched buildings once stood. The column was erected in 1852 as a monument to the Duke of Wellington at the urging of Major Richardes of Bryneithin, a Waterloo veteran[56]. It represents a cannon pointing skywards and was meant to have been topped by a mounted man, probably Wellington himself, but this never came about. To persuade townsfolk to pay for the construction of the monument it was suggested that the sight of the Iron Duke even in effigy would've been enough to discourage sea-borne invaders. Perhaps just a giant tallywhacker does the same job.

It's great up here, on this high hill, above the town, where people once lived and loved and laboured. I spent many a slow dole day up here, years ago; many books were read. It's kind of comforting, the presence of this hill, visible from almost anywhere in the town; the knowledge that it'll always be here, easily accessible and forever redolent of summer, is comforting. So the fort still fulfils its function.

At the hill's foot, on the once-inhabited coastal plain, the information board tells me that I'm standing on the best example of a vegetated spit in Ceredigion. The blackthorn trees here are estimated to be over two centuries old. It's amazingly fecund; there's yellow rattle, knotted hedge-parsley, oatgrass. Peacock butterflies flap from flower to flower to feed. Ravens croak at each other on the lower slopes of Pen Dinas; choughs have been seen; kingfishers, too, on the Rheidol, which acted as a natural moat. Sparrowhawks hunt. Oystercatchers and ringed plover wander up from the beach and stonechats and pipits flit through the gorse. Watch the wheatears whir away from you and you'll understand why they were given that name (it's an endearing corruption of 'white arse'). In the summer months,

trotting races and clay-pigeon shoots are held on the somewhat boggy field between the fort and Allt Wen. Not long ago, this area would reek from the landfill. You'd taste it. Your eyes would water. The air would shimmer with methane from rot and not much moved but rats and gulls and flies. That's changed.

PENGLAIS HILL: UNIVERSITY/ARTS CENTRE AND NATIONAL LIBRARY

Ah, the Nat Lib. Vast presence on its perch glaring down at the never-to-be-educated town below. Both cathedral to learning and Kafka's Castle[57]. Where to start with it? It dominates all of the town's cultural institutions and enterprises, including the one you're reading right now. It's colossal.

I worked there for a while, some years ago, during the extensive renovations and updates. I was given the job of demolishing the room used to house rare books; an early edition of *The Canterbury Tales*, supposedly, and also of *The Black Book of Carmarthen* ('worth a million quid, they reckon', went the gossip over tea and butties and roll-ups in the site canteen). The room was bomb-proof; concrete walls three feet thick, reinforced by high tensile steel. My workmate and I were given various tools with which to do the job; a hammer and bolster, a grinder, and three different sizes of jackhammer. The only thing which made any impression on the walls was the biggest jackhammer, a 75 lb behemoth that often had to be held up above the head. Ten hour shifts. Dawn 'til dusk. Utterly exhausting work, and badly paid, too. It left me traumatised somewhat, and although I no longer involuntarily flinch and wince when I hear a pneumatic drill start up in the street, I do get taken back to the days when, if I wasn't juddering in every muscle and bone in choking dust and racket for hours at a time, I was sleeping off the exertion of doing so, and that's a place I'd rather leave behind[58]. Still, it's a stunning building now, both inside and out, and I helped it get that way. A small contribution, admittedly, but nevertheless.

This year, 2007, is the library's centenary. Beatrice Davies, secretary to the very first librarian, died only last year, aged 102. In *Born on a Perilous Rock*, W.J. Lewis describes how the library had its genesis in Clerkenwell Green, in London, in the mid eighteenth century, when the Society of Antient (sic) Britons provided for a library at the Welsh School there which was intended to house a copy of every book printed in Welsh and as many manuscripts as could be acquired in any other language. Iolo Morgannwg (more on whom soon) may have made the first mention of a National Library in his will, in which he left his archive to such an institution providing it was set up before 1820, but it didn't receive serious consideration until 1873, at the National Eisteddfod in Mold, when Sir Hugh Owen and Stephen Evans set up a committee to consider the matter. Manuscripts were at that point stored in the college in Aberystwyth, but the 1885 fire re-arranged priorities, as flame tends to do. The idea wasn't forgotten, though, and when the then Chancellor of the Exchequer hinted at the availability of funds in 1904 a collection was quickly amassed; Sir John Williams and Sir Henry Owen, amongst others, promised to donate their own libraries, and canvassed support country-wide for the library to be based in Aberystwyth, and not Cardiff. The smaller mid-Wales town was seen as being more Welsh than the big southern city, which 'had not much that was Welsh in spirit'. The central location, too, was favourable, as was the availability of a fourteen-acre site, and in June 1905 the Privy Council declared that Aber could have the Library, and Cardiff the National Museum; Lewis digs up a tremendous quote from the *Western Mail* concerning this decision, that it would be 'a permanent reminder of the inability of Wales to agree on any question of national importance, because of the rival jealousies which had been the greatest enemies of Welsh nationalism in the past'. By, but how things change, ey?

Anyway. The celebratory procession dissolved into a shambles, with the *Cambrian News* labelling it 'altogether... the poorest procession Aberystwyth has ever seen', and the Library received its Charter of Incorporation from King Edward VII in 1907. The foundation stone was laid by King George V and Queen Mary on 15th July 1911; the regal couple were greeted at the train station by the Moelwyn Choir accompanied by a Royal Navy band and the Royal Carriage was escorted to the Library site by a troop of Household Cavalry in full uniform. The king laid the stone. Eight warships in the bay fired a twenty-one-gun salute.

Good Lord. This is all true.

So the Library – by now deserving of its capitalisation – went up. And up and up and out and out. Further royal visits followed on 16th July 1937, when George VI and Queen Elizabeth opened the new Central Block, and on 8th August 1955 when the Queen and Duke of Edinburgh opened the final section, according to the original plans. A fourth visit in more recent years was cut short due to protestors; the royal cortege was egged, on the approach road to the Library. As we know, that's the only occasion when the Queen has had to cut short a royal visit. The National Library has become a political edifice as much as a cultural one. And it's all the stronger for that.

Amongst the Library's acquisitions, Lewis writes, are the *Black Book of Carmarthen*, 'the oldest MS in the Welsh language', and the Hengwrt *Chaucer*. So maybe the rumours were true. Its growth rate is in the region of 45,000 new items each year, and a current project is to digitally store the entire archive, an immense undertaking[59]. Head of digital developments is Rocet Arwel Jones, and I meet him up at the Library on a rainy day, which means we can't sit outside and admire the view over the town and the bay.

Opposite to Arianrhod in *The Mabinogion*, who has no name, Rocet has several; his given one is Robert, but he tells me that his big nose prompted the nickname 'Rocet' (his hooter seems a modest size to me). He's also a travel writer and poet (his *Jumbo Caribou*, published by Y Lolfa, is about his travels across Kenya) who's been to Peru (I'm envious) and is going to Kyrgyztan later this year (2007). He was born on Ynys Môn, came to Aberystwyth in 1986 to study, and never left. He swore to himself that he'd never work in the National Library 'because it's full of weird people', but he did, and does; he began working with early Welsh manuscripts, then literary archives, then acquisitions (maps, manuscripts, basically everything that wasn't printed). He talks about the Mary Dillwyn Llewelyn archive, which contains some of the earliest photographs taken by a woman in Wales, and how it was initially bought by a museum in the States, but Rocet succeeded in getting an export ban put on it, thereby saving it for Wales. He's now helping to digitally store 600,000 pages of Welsh journals since 1900 (*Barn, Dock Leaves*, Kiedrych Rhys' *Wales, Planet* etc.). There's a copyright problem – he might need to contact each one of 50,000 authors or their descendants – but the project will facilitate amazing ease of research. There's also the 'Wales-Ohio' project, the goal of which is to 'digitize a selection of Welsh Americana relating to the state of Ohio... and to make [it] available on a bilingual website', according to the promotional leaflet I pick up; there'll be photographs, maps, prints and paintings, 'giving a taste of what life was like to the Welsh settlers in the nineteenth century.... It will also celebrate and strengthen the bonds that exist between Wales and Ohio' (same leaflet). It's been partly funded by Evan and Elizabeth Davies of Oak Hill, 'well-known benefactors of America's Welsh heritage'.

We talk more. Rocet sees a Celtic triangle between Aberystwyth, Galway, and, surprisingly, Freiburg in Germany, which has a Welsh language school: 'I can imagine the same sort of people, or even the same people, appearing in all three places'[60]. And the Welshness of Aberystwyth? 'There's a few weeks in the year when it surfaces, before Christmas when there's no Brummies or students'. He says that a lot of Aber's Welsh speakers are incomers from other parts of

Wales, but he's also noticed that a lot of people are returning to the town to open shops and cafés etc (both Dots and the Blue Creek caff are run by Aber-born Welsh speakers). He sees in this a new 'entrepreneurial' element in Welsh life[61], which feeds back into the digitalisation project; Welsh people globally now have access to all manner of useful data. The isolation of Aber, Rocet says, has forced on it a cosmopolitan mindset; in Bangor, say, you could study there and live in Pwllheli or Chester, 'but the fact that students and non-students have to learn to live with each other gives Aber its life'.

He's comfortable and invigorating company, Rocet is. I could blether with him all day, but we've both got work to do, so I leave him to get on with his and take a wander about the Library's interior, through the exhibits, picking up leaflets as I go. There's a world of stuff happening in here, and I gather to me enough promotional material as to constitute a small archive in itself; there's *Gwladfa Kyffin*, a travelling exhibition organised by the National Library of the photographs the artist Kyffin Williams took on his trip to Patagonia in 1968, and of the paintings he made on his return to these shores; there's the 'Myths, Memories and Futures' Centenary Lecture Series, which considered the ways in which those three things inter-mingle in the parallel stories of the National Library and the National Museum in Cardiff; there's a new film festival, to take place in October 2007, organised by the National Screen and Sound Archive of Wales, entitled 'Wales Screen Classics' and to include *Y Chwarelwr, How Green was my Valley, The Life Story of David Lloyd George* and rare footage from William Haggar; there's a 'Guide to Sources' pertaining to the 'Family History' database (parish registers, diocesan records, census returns etc.); and a great deal more. The building is huge, incorporating a restaurant, various permanent exhibitions, a main hall, council chambers, two reading rooms, a gallery and an upper hall in the Drwm, which is a 100-seater auditorium used for conferences, screenings, and readings etc. It's a big, vibrant, inquisitive place, a monument to learning and communicating; some of the best minds that have ever existed can be freely contacted here. Items in the collection are uncountable, despite the best efforts of professional thieves like Peter Bellwood, 'who disguised himself as a bumbling academic to take thousands of rare maps, [and] was jailed in 2004 for stealing fifty... from the National Library of Wales in Aberystwyth'[62]. The Library's a fortress, but I wonder more about the 'why' than the 'how'; did he plan to sell them? Or just sit and stare at them by candlelight? What more did he hope to gain through possession of these singular artefacts? Odd, and of a piece with those who collect the eggs of rare birds. Unfathomable desires.

The Library's brightest jewel in this centenary year seems to be its Iolo Morgannwg archive, which Trevor Fishlock, on a BBC2 Wales feature about this very collection, called 'the outpourings of a volcanic mind'. Morgannwg, according to Fishlock, was 'a rescuer and champion of his country's culture, a prospector who always found gold'. He was baptised Edward Williams, but changed his name to sound more Cymric, and his works on bardic and druidic lore were, at first, suspect; in fact, they'd be seen as a Chattertonian or Ossianian hoax were it not for his other achievements, so instead they're referred to as 'a Wales of the imagination, [described] in a river of unrestrained writing'. Of course.

In truth, Morgannwg is a towering, beguiling figure. As well as his 're-creations', he was a forger of coins, a tireless note-taker, and a keen naturalist who regularly walked thirty miles or so in a day, scribbling as he went, so his archive is a rich mine of period information. His *Secrets of the Bards of the Isle of Britain* was written whilst in debtor's prison; people, needing the grounding of tangible cultural history, wanted dearly to believe in its authenticity, so that's exactly what they did, and do. Mary-Anne Constantine, who is responsible for the creation and upkeep of the archive, stated, on the BBC2 Wales programme referred to above, that 'he had a vision of the past which needs to be embodied', and the historian[63] John Davies (ditto) points out that Shakespeare did a similar thing: 'improving, adding, and enriching'. Unlike Shakespeare, though, Iolo was a junkie – a keen consumer of laudanum, for fifty years, first experimented with as a potential cure for his asthma. On his return to London in 1791, he found that his words wouldn't flow, there was a costive block, so he took yet more of the drug and had some kind of breakdown; the letters to his wife from this period are full of terror and suicidal impulses and references to this 'good-for-nothing world'. He recovered, however, and later put the crisis down to 'an inflammation of the brain' brought on by sunbathing. Silly bugger.

His greatest creation, of course, was the gorsedd of bards, first staged in 1792 at Primrose Hill in London, and which became transplanted into the eisteddfod later that decade. He invented a complete bardic script, which wasn't examined or questioned largely because his inventions were, at the time, deeply attractive to Wales and its people, who were needing to believe that they had a living culture far older than anything England, perfidious Albion, could ever dream about. John Davies points to the stabilising influence of this at a time of rapid and profound change, and how invention becomes reality, and Mary-Anne Constantine, in an (at the time of writing) unpublished essay 'In a Very Deranged State: Notes on the Iolo Morgannwg Project', talks about the untramelled nature of the man's manuscripts, how they leap from subject to subject, how he appears like a never-satiated spider at the centre of a vast web of learning:

> Science? There's the medicinal visit in 1792 to one 'Mr Long Operator in Electricity in Compton Street, Soho, who electrified me, drawing sparks repeatedly from my hands, arms, breast, knees'. Geology? The cliffs of Glamorgan yielded 'the head of a small horned animal petrified in a quarry of limerock. I suppose that it must have been a fish'. Urban versus pastoral? 'Let those that abide in the filth of a town/Deride, if they please, the meek life of a clown'.

And so on, 'creations [that] fed directly into Welsh historiography, and helped shape the modern nation in its formative stages'[64].

A John Osmond-edited anthology of essays appeared in January 2007, entitled *Myths, Memories and Futures*, transcripts of the Centenary Lecture Series mentioned earlier. Many of the pieces touch on the political aspects of the Library; Rhiannon Mason remarks how British MPs, in the late 1890s, were aghast at Welsh MPs declaring their intention of setting up a National Library, because, in their eyes, Wales already had one, in South Kensington. The establishment of the Library, and the Museum, 'signified a new acceptance that Wales's history and culture could henceforth not be simply subsumed within Britain's cultural institutions. By creating its own national institutions, Wales both won – and was granted – official recognition for its national distinctiveness'. Following on from this, in the same anthology, Andrew Green writes: 'There is still room... for an institution that welcomes unconditionally, that speaks without preaching or expecting payment, that enriches our common human experience, that hands on our inheritance to our successors'.

Remember: most civic buildings in Wales aren't simply housing for offices or documents – identity politics mortars them all. Last word on the Library can go, again, to Gwyneth Lewis, who, in her Ph.D., did some pioneering work on the Morgannwg archive. Her poem, commissioned by the Library for the centenary celebrations, reads:

Centenary Greetings from the National Library of Wales

We call, as one lighthouse hails another
by sight, through the electronic dark.
Digital seeds stir in our nation's ark.

Hidden most safely is the DNA
of dreams in vellum, which the warble fly
has tasted, so knows where all our bodies lie.

Ideas' spores are spread by the eyes
of greedy readers who, randy as bees,
nudge the dusty interstices

of images until they pollinate
towering pistils. Some metaphors bloom
only once a century in tradition's gloom.

Some books, like poodles, are sent to be groomed
in the binding department, till their spines
are tongues again and can speak their mind.

The hardest place to be is here,
we need to imagine it and require
a library's wormholes, its infinite doors.

A short walk up Penglais Hill will take you to the newer campus of the university. It's much like any other post-war further education establishment, if one reads 'greyblock' for 'redbrick', but there is a bell tower that resembles a giant Stanley knife and a strange sculpture of a concrete staircase to nowhere that the *Cambrian Snooze* explains as a forward-thinking seating area 'from which to observe yachting regattas and the like' when global warming has turned the campus into part of Aber's promenade in a few decades' time. There's an Arts Centre here too, apparently the largest in Wales, which houses the Ceramics Collection, a Great Hall, a bookshop, CD racks, and a couple of bars and a good restaurant, where I join Jem Poster for a bowl of bean stew. Jem's Professor of Creative Writing up here, and is the author of two superb, mud-drenched historical novels, *Courting Shadows* and *Rifling Paradise*. He's been in Aber since 2003, and says

he finds space and time here to write, 'a different kind of busy-ness' to what he experienced in Oxford. He was under commission to work on William Golding and Virginia Woolf but the urge to make his own novel became too strong, and the historical settings of his two books so far are concomitant with his training in archeology, from which he earned a living in the 1970s. *Courting Shadows*, his first novel, was written in a converted chapel outside Machynlleth. I ask him whether the country he lives in influences his work in any way and he answers 'Wales is there', which is enough. Read his books – if you haven't already – and see for yourself.

Parthian Books have an office up here, recently relocated from Pier Street, as does *New Welsh Review*, whose editor, Francesca Rhydderch, joins me a few minutes after Jem leaves. Another one to interrogate. Place is full of them. Fran was born in Aber, but brought up in Newquay. Her father was a seafarer. She lived in Llanelli between the ages of eight and seventeen but worked her way back into Aber through university. Her sister, Samantha, accomplished and interesting poet, still lives in Newquay. Did Aber exert a pull? 'Well, Ceredigion and the sea did. It felt like I was coming home and this is where I'll stay'. She took over *NWR* in 2002, which, before that, she says, was very much a Cardiff magazine, and she was well aware that she was shifting it from that centre – it was a conscious decision. She's made big editorial changes, which was easier to do in a more remote place such as Aber. Some of these changes have been rather offensive to a reactionary and foursquare type of person (which is never a bad response to provoke from such people); Fran felt that the magazine needed more of 'a creative heart' to reflect a culture that was becoming more mature and confident, 'not just absorbing outside influences but inviting people here'. The approach seems to have worked; the readership is increasing, with a 5 per cent shift from within Wales to outside it – new readers are being drawn in and caught. *NWR* isn't part of a clique, but new writers are starting to cluster around it, a develop-ment more organic than organised, and being based in Aber, Fran feels, has helped this to happen; edgy places attract similar voices.

And it's brilliant, I think, what Fran's done with *NWR*. Wales was crying out for that kind of forum, for a magazine with pedigree and authority to take a creative risk and to acknowledge the sharper and harder voices that were beginning to shout at the turn of this century. The creative languages in Wales – or rather, those with English as a parent – were becoming stale and uninteresting and too besotted with precedent, and these were the voices that were being heard, that were being listened to, that were being allowed to communicate experiences and knowledge of a Wales utterly unrecognisable to the millions who lived outside of academia and conservatories. I'm pleased to see that stranglehold being loosened. Fran's editorship of the magazine was one catalyst for that, outlet as it suddenly was, and the recent guest editors – Tristan Hughes and Patrick McGuinness, to name but two – are sustaining the impetus[65]. Long may it continue.

So, Fran; Aberystwyth. Is it arty and bohemian? Do you find it so? Fran replies that she does, but finds it 'also very middle-class', as exemplified in the university and the Library. It's not as bohemian as people might think it is, which isn't a value judgement, she says, 'simply an observation'. Does it breed artistic behaviour? Well, Ceredigion itself does – look at Caryl Lewis (we will, later), and Mihangel Morgan (we already have), for example. 'There's definitely something here that fosters creativity, if not breeds it. Good art in Aber is very accessible; it can be seen in many places, for free. There's a small population but a huge arts centre. The town is quietly creative... there's a buzz, but a background buzz. It never delivers itself in just one way. Small towns provoke honesty... one can't be anonymous in them'.

Fran's husband, Damien Walford Davies, lectures in the English department on Romanticism but also edits anthologies and has a poetry collection out with Parthian, called *Whiteout*, co-authored with Richard Marggraf Turley (Damien has a solo collection with Seren appearing in 2009). When Fran's gone, I pick up a copy from the bookshop and flip through it and it's immediately striking, the care for language, the tastes and sounds of words. Echoes of Antony Barnett or Thomas A. Clark, but filtered through a different sensibility; more biological, perhaps. Look:

M4

I'll tell you what
alien is:

                    that night-
          drift west from
          Cardiff, constellated
          tankers pushing
          to their chevroned exits.

For a while I'm happy up here, with poetry and coffee on my own.
But then the setting – the university – begins to intrude. All around
me is earnest thesis talk and it starts to get to me. I can see over the
entire town from up here, out to the sea. The roof of Pantycelyn Hall
gleams wetly below; I think of how taxi drivers are loath to take
students there because nine times out of ten they do a runner on the
three quid fare, and of how, last year, the flower-boxes on the promenade were overturned and smashed to bits by Pantycelyn students[66].
There are undoubtedly many decent people in that hall, and in all the
others, and students will be students and all that shite, but my mood
has suddenly plummeted. Besides which, I long ago drifted away
from academia, as I drifted from the general society of singular-
purposed humankind (largely; there are exceptions). I feel
uncomfortable here, amongst this talk and these people. I've gone too
far away from them to ever feel entirely at ease in their company
anymore. I'll take *Whiteout* elsewhere. I'm off. Inland.

Notes

1   Sic. Kessinger, who publish the book, specialize in re-printing 'thousands of hard-to-find
    books!', to quote the fly-leaf, complete with exclamation mark, but supply no bibliographi
    cal information – no date, no source. But there's an undeniably Victorian feel to Howells's
    prose.
2   We've been there too, haven't we? Imagine them there, Powell and Swinburne and this odd
    foppish Yankee, in amongst the ghosts. The flagellation and the fawning and the oh-so-sensi
    tive swoons. Brrr.
3   No, second; the first was an impromptu support slot to the great poet Tom Pickard on the
    Penglais campus, from a proof copy of my first novel, a few months before publication.
4   Fine local writers and people whom you'll meet later.
5   *Perilous Rock*, of course.
6   Founder of the modern Baptists, 1554-1612.
7   St. Brieuc, in Brittany, is one of Aberystwyth's twin towns.
8   National Library archivist, Welsh-language poet and travel-writer, explorer and fine fellow.
9   This can be found in the collection *People and Places*. See 'Works Consulted'.
10 A souk bar? A dispensary of strong alcohol named after a Moslem bazaar? Yes, I see the
    link...
11 The specific reference for which I've lost. I do apologise.

12 See website www.thecarvery.net.
13 Interesting how fire keeps trying to lay claim to this town of many waters.
14 I've been told that the Sex Pistols played there too, but I've been unable to corroborate that.
15 'Harsh Hill', an accurate piece of nomenclature if ever there was one.
16 Where, oddly, I find a raw prawn on the rocks in mid-stream.
17 Cwmrheidol, where we'll spend more time later.
18 Llangranog, an extremely pretty seaside village twenty miles or so south of Aberystwyth, is one favoured summer camp.
19 For further details, see the 'Urdd' section in *Born on a Perilous Rock*.
20 See *Perilous Rock*.
21 In the *Cambrian News* article 'Sea-front may soon be a distant memory'. See 'Works Consulted'.
22 An oneiric Aber, an Aber that only partly has an index in reality. But nonetheless. . .
23 Sic again; I wish the title would change, too. But it's not going to.
24 Okay, I retract; he doesn't get gushy about the castle at all.
25 This is calculable because extensive accounts still survive; every half penny spent was recorded.
26 Llywernog, for example, the precious metal from which gives Bwlch Nant yr Arian – which we'll visit later – its name.
27 Who, to be fair, is now an effective heritage campaigner.
28 From 'My Emphasis' in *Seven Tales of Sex and Death*.
29 Still, there's the proximity of the playground to be taken into consideration. Time and place and all that. This isn't it.
30 See the terribly moving last chapter in *Neighbours from Hell*.
31 Meaning the generic 'high street', not the real-life High Street, on the corner of which the Ship and Castle pub stands.
32 All quotes from personal emails, unless indicated otherwise.
33 'Brook of the Prairie', bafflingly.
34 Called *Kink and Particle*.
35 In *To Dream of Freedom*.
36 And there are many, in this town as in all others.
37 If this were Australia, Great Darkgate Street would be Aber's CBD – Central Business District. But it's not. So it isn't. Count your blessings.
38 See *Presenting Saunders Lewis* in 'Works Consulted'.
39 See John Harris's superb introduction to *Fury Never Leaves Us*, in 'Works Consulted'.
40 See Afterword to *Morgan Bible and Journals 1939-1944* in 'Works Consulted'.
41 Included in *The Earth Gives All and Takes All*.
42 See *Morgan Bible*.
43 The money, of course, was all Marguerite's.
44 Or so says Andrew Lycett, in his biography of Thomas; Paul Ferris is a lot less generous about the episode. See 'Works Consulted'.
45 The discussion of the reasons for which would make up a different and separate book. Which will have to wait.
46 I have, and find both cities to be unrelaxed, tense, wound-up, Perth maybe the moreso of the two, even. But maybe that's just me.
47 Not in western Australia, in my experience. But now I'm repeating myself. I'll leave it be.
48 Quoted in Jim Perrin, *Travels With the Flea*. 'Works Consulted'.
49 See Richard Holland, *Wales of the Unexpected*, 'Works Consulted'.
50 In huge letters on the outside of the Millennium Building in Cardiff Bay. I'm not going to tell you what those five words are, if you don't know. Go and see for yourself.

51   Quote from a personal conversation.
52   Gwyneth emailed it to me, but it has been published in *Planet*, although I've been unable to ascertain exactly when.
53   And there, if the novel is anything to go by, become genitally obsessed, pederastically minded, tinged with a misogynistic disgust, and salaciously drawn to transexualism and urophilia. If that's your bag as well, then the novel's a rattling read.
54   See *Chaotic Angels*, 'Works Consulted'.
55   I looked at one or two with an eye-to-buy but the space-to-money ratio had me scarpering into the hills. Ludicrous situation.
561   I've heard that it was physically constructed by one man with one arm and a donkey, but I've been unable to verify that. Apocryphal, probably.
57   Malcolm Pryce, in his *Aberystwyth Mon Amour*, has a brilliant take on the library as a sinister place that only a select cabal of initiates can enter, which is of course fictitious; the staff are, in truth, helpful and friendly and approachable. But it's an amusing idea.
58   I was working on my first novel at the time, too. Where did that energy go? It's salutary, I feel, for an aspirant writer to undertake such paid work, for reasons too many to go into here. But that said, I wouldn't've done it, had I had the choice.
59   The website – llgc.org.uk – is easily navigable, but beware; you could spend days wandering around it. It's fascinating.
60   Personally, I would've replaced Freiburg with Lublin (in Poland), but anyway.
61   We have a laugh over the Englishman, quoted in Mike Parker's *Neighbours from Hell*, who sneered at the fact that the Welsh language, unlike the English, has no word for 'entrepreneur'. Oaf.
62   See Patrick Barkham's 2006 *Guardian* article in 'Works Consulted'.
63   An invaluable Aber fixture; John was on Trefechan Bridge that day in 1962, remember?
64   Mary-Anne's essay, and another, utterly absorbing piece by her called 'Seeing Daylight All the Way: Notes on Sleep from Iolo's Manuscripts', are to be published in a composite volume later this year (2007). If you can't wait til then, there is, of course, the digital archive.
65   Patrick's based in academia, of course. But of a different sort to what went before.
66   Pantycelyn is a Welsh-language only hall, so I'm sure such vandalism came out of patriotic love and pride.

HINTERLANDS

PENRHYNCOCH

I like it here. I'm relaxed. Small, quiet village in a bowl of hills, close enough to Aberystwyth for the town's glow to be visible over the hill-tops at night-time, yet far enough away for it to feel less like a suburb of the town and more of a remote, self-contained little civic centre in itself. There's a village square with a war memorial – terribly sad, as such things always are; the devastation – and general store, a garage with another shop attached, a footy club with a bar, big screen, pool table and food, numerous places of worship, and a couple of estates which sprung up in the 60s and turned the place from an isolated hamlet into a dormitory village for Aberystwyth, a few miles away over the hill. The people here are a special breed; approachable, warm, friendly, quick and eager to help. I like it here.

Dafydd ap Gwilym was born here. A sign in the car park of the village hall points down a lane; follow it for a mile or so and you'll come to a mound of mouldy boulders in a private garden. That's where Wales's greatest medieval poet came into the world seven centuries ago. There's a plaque of commemoration, and that's it, although there has been talk recently of opening a Dafydd ap Gwilym centre in Penrhyncoch, complete with exhibition, retail outlet, library, video and film facilities, and lecture theatre. God knows where it'd go; any open land around the village belongs to a working farm. The *Cambrian News* of November 2nd 2006 carried a small article about this venture, in which MP Mark Williams gave his backing to it and stated that Dafydd 'embodies what we in Wales in the twenty-first century must strive to celebrate and honour', although what that might particularly be, I

haven't a clue, but I suspect it's got nothing to do with the urge to build the centre in the first place. Since that article appeared, I haven't heard anything about the project. Maybe plans are being drawn up in offices somewhere. We have Dafydd's birthplace, his grave (in Ystrad Fflur), and of course his work, in various editions. Do we really need anything more? Isn't that enough? Art, it seems, needs validation through touch-technology; buttons to press, mouses to click. The original beauty of its venture isn't enough, anymore.

It's wet, today. Rain has been falling steadily for hours and everything seems sodden. Hills like great green sponges. Cows with drooping quiffs stare and chew over gates. Sheep, even at my approach, refuse to shift from the patches of dry ground on which they're lying. Suggestions of discarded perukes in a judge's chambers. The soft lilac flowers of cranesbill on one of the surrounding slopes have been robbed by the rain of most colour and hawthorn and cow parsley and oxeye daisies all wilt in the wet. The sky is one grey and the air is broth-thick, narcotic. Turning a corner between dripping hedges I disturb a sparrowhawk on the road; it shoots upwards and circles squealing whilst I examine what was occupying it so: A finch, perfectly plucked except for the head, a little ball of grey goose-bumped flesh, feet skywards, tiny eyes closed, a rim of blood at the beak. I leave the hawk to its dinner, and further down the lane, closer to the village, come across another dead bird on the glistening tarmac – a seagull, but so mutilated as to be barely recognisable as such; guts spilling, head half gone, patches of torn flesh where the quills have been wrenched. A big bird like a gull? Fox, maybe. But I can't smell the spoor, and I can feel eyes on me, so I look up, and there on top of a telegraph pole is the gull's killer; bluey-grey stripes, navy head out of which yellow eyes are locked on my face. Tensed, focussed, ferocious. Peregrine falcon. No wonder no birds are singing[1].

I need shelter (although, to be honest, I can't get any wetter than I am without drowning), so I duck into Eglwys Sant Ioan to dry off. It's a magnificent church, consecrated in 1881 after services were held in the day school[2], under the supervision and oversight of the church at Llanbadarn Fawr. The first precentor (or 'codwr canu', literally 'lifter of song') was a Mr. John Jones of Pompren Court, wherever that is. Funds for the church were raised by Sir Pryse of Gogerddan. The first to get married here were Elizabeth Owen of Cwmbwa Mill and Michael Bowen of Machynlleth, on October 26 , 1881, and the first to be christened was

Samuel Magor of Garth in the same year. I hope their lives were happy and good. The St. John of the church's name is St. John of God, also called John the Apostle, author of the Fourth Gospel (and, some think, The Book of Revelations), patron of theologians, writers, and 'all who work at the production of books'[3]. Seems apt. So I'm sheltered from more than rain in the doorway of his house.

There's an interesting painting on the wall in the church, made, to celebrate the 125th anniversary of the church's consecration, by Margaret Jones of Capel Bangor. It's a large watercolour, a mélange of historical figures and events of local significance and connection. Framing it are representations of the Celtic crosses at Llanbadarn; there's St. Padarn himself, who appears to be shooing birds with his staff, I don't know why; Dafydd ap Gwilym sits on a mound and strums a lute; there's Lewis Morris, who lived nearby at Capel Madog; and there are scenes of mining, hunting, smelting. It's a rich area, this. IGER – the Institute of Grassland and Environmental Research – has a large complex at the entrance to the village. It's a big employer, and important research establishment to do with agricultural yields and that kind of thing, but funding problems have beset it in recent years. A tad too boring to look at in any depth, really.

It's still raining when I leave the church and I can't, through the drifting curtains of wet, see the mountain that rises up over the village. But I know it's there.

PENDAM

This is an intriguing, beguiling mountain. It's not especially high, being really the foothills of the greater hump of Pumlumon[4], but it's wide, and the sense of surrounding space when on it is enormous. It's crowned by Nordic-looking lakes and pinewoods. Aberystwyth is visible on a clear day, as is the Llŷn peninsula and, on rare occasions, Ireland. There are standing stones and ruins. Bogs and great grey fins of jagged rock. Scattered hamlets, too, still inhabited, the first of which as you climb up from Penrhyncoch is Penrhiw-newydd, a wind-battered handful of stone houses with spectacular views, front and back. A terribly sad story clings to this place, concerning a suicide pact between two elderly and reclusive people, aged eighty-five and eighty-seven, seven years ago. The male half of the couple – let's

call him Bob – slashed the wrists of his wife and then did the same to himself. She died, but he survived, and was put on probation for three years after admitting to manslaughter. They were so reclusive that when their names were released, nobody had the faintest idea who they were, even in a hamlet as tiny as this one. Bob would go to another village to shop and collect his pension and when his car needed servicing he'd leave it at the end of the lane for the garage to collect. It came out in court that the couple were terrified of losing their home due to illness, Bob's wife having suffered for years from heart disease, arthritis, and bronchitis, with Bob himself falling into despair at the thought of life without her. Diminished responsibility, said the judge. Probation. Leniency.

It's a heartbreaking story. That's not just ghosts or only the wind you can hear wailing throughout the long unlit nights on these naked and scoured peaks, close to the dark and twinkling sky under which all things move in innocence. And at the site of the old mine above the even smaller hamlet of Llwyn Prysg, the pump sunk in the earth by the stream is still working; you can hear it rhythmically thumping in the earth, the mountain's heartbeat, stricken and yearning. At the top of the cataract here, as night falls, you can see Aberystwyth's lights flickering yellowly on. And you can feel infinitely more than a mere few miles away from their warm glow in this gouged and wild and beating place.

Indeed, mines thread and runnel these hills like the tunnels of earthworms in a tank of soil. Silver, lead and copper were mined here from prehistory to the turn of the twentieth century. The villages of Cwmsymlog, Cwmerfyn and Pen-bont Rhydybeddau housed the earth-workers and their families, but all facilities have now gone – no shops or pubs or chapels, although a couple of schools still function, and the communities exude an air of resilient liveliness. Objective 1 funding has assisted the establishment of the 'Spirit of the Miners' project; according to the spring 2006 newsletter, '£300,000 is available to voluntary/community groups, Community Councils, existing or new businesses and public sector organisations looking to make a difference in their areas by using the heritage of our past metal mining industry as a theme for regeneration'[5]. In practice, this means tapping into the touristic and educational potential of mining's legacy; constructing exhibitions, creating tours etc., turning the rusting machinery and empty shells of buildings into promotable and marketable objects of interest. It's a good idea, in many ways, not least because these sites' geological peculiarities, as well as their unique flora, need to be appreciated and preserved. Better to utilise the ruins, in this case, than let them rot, and the echoes of an entire way of life rot with them. In truth, though, I haven't, personally, seen much evidence of this happening, apart from the scaffolding that surrounds the chimney at Cwmsymlog, but of course that's not to say that it isn't going on. Or going to go on. Maybe I miss too much.

People lived in these hills long before they ever thought to extract minerals from them on a large scale. At Banc y Darren, another hamlet built and battered on an exposed ridge[6], archaeologists in 2005 unearthed a grand gateway entrance into a hill fort dating back 2,500 years. This gateway was pillared and contained a quartz boulder that probably expressed power[7], a status symbol, a prehistoric BMW. The inhabitants, it's thought, were a group of lower rank than those based at Pen Dinas, visible from here. Isn't it incredible, what boils in these hills beneath your boots? I try to imagine their lives here, all those years ago, but can't, really; my mind's crowded with thoughts of food and research and whether Pulsar will be able to detect and eradicate the virus in my laptop in time for me to file copy by tomorrow evening. Sometimes such stuff can't be banished. It nags and niggles and won't leave you alone.

But it's still, up here. The world has a stillness and quietude to it that it doesn't tend to have on lower ground. Little moves but the air, lightly, and a small bird in the bare branches of a bent and blackened tree. He too is hungry. John Barnie has written of this place that 'in such a still world the eye follows anything that moves'[8], and whereas for him it was an out-of-control Phantom drone, for me, today, it's the flailing sails of the windmills on the far side of the valley, right next to where the treeline – all pine, of course – begins. Now here's something to get concerned about; two things, in fact. In *Neighbours from Hell*, Mike Parker refers to the conifer plantations as 'green concrete'[9]; there are some good reasons for re-foresting some parts of Wales with this crop, Mike says, but

> the angular giants... have been allowed to run riot over huge swathes of the country, [and] a clearer symbol of rural subjugation and marginalisation it would be harder to find. They are... nature at its most unnatural, choking to a swift and relentless death everything that once grew beneath them. Even when the trees are felled, there's nothing but a desolate wasteland left behind.

And then there's the wind turbines, scores of which are visible from these peaks, their blades front-crawling above the distant ridges. Again, there's something to be said for Wales shouldering, or rather sharing, some of the burden for renewable energy, but, to quote Mike again, 'it threatens to get out of hand....Wales, with 8.5 per cent of the UK's total landmass and around 5 per cent of [its] population, is home to almost 50 per cent of the UK's wind turbines'. They're not negligible statistics; they say something about the exploitative attitudes of a colonial power towards it's territories, and whilst the turbines don't pose the same immediate physical danger as say, the slag heap did above Aberfan in the 1960s, they're still of a piece with policies which are, at best, diffident and, at worse, criminally irresponsible; blight the hills above Chequers or Sandringham with these spindly, ugly, dominant things? Monoculture-ise the hills around Balmoral with one tree specie only? Allow a teetering mound of sodden slag to grow above Eton or Harrow?

Jim Perrin has written with brilliant and angry eloquence about the espoliation of once-wild Wales. It's about time you were introduced to Jim, if you don't know him or his work already; mountaineer, traveller, essayist, biographer, journalist, and one of the loveliest, bravest men I know. The way he's

borne terrible recent bereavements with a kind of longing, grateful
stoicism, has moved, impressed and guided me and will continue to
do so for as long as I'm alive (maybe afterwards, too). He knows the
mountains of mid-Wales as much as anyone ever could, and his
marrow-deep love and respect for them underpins much of his lucid
and startling writing[10]. He contributes regularly to the *Guardian*'s
'Country Diary' column, and in March of 2007 he wrote about
camping on Pumlumon Fawr (see next chapter) and waking to see
'hundreds of wind turbines' on the ridges. 'The MSPs,' he writes,
'should come here to see how completely these presences destroy the
sense of wildness that is crucial to our wellbeing. You can't argue with
its proponent's basic intentions, but wind technology is inappropriate
for Britain's last wild places – a plain moral fact about a crucial spiritual resource that governments and "green" zealots must heed before
the land is entirely lost'[11].

It's important, I think, that we recognise this. I've never taken the
Bill McKibben stance[12], that what we now know as 'nature' is little
more than a cognitive construct created by folk-memory and TV
programming and by what we want or need to believe is beyond our
front doors (spend a night on a mountain and you'll realize that
imaginary entities don't bite or blast or soak or bake you), but the
proliferation of wind farms in this area as in others is beginning to
move us towards that; a place in which man's technological obsession
and imperiousness is so blaring and conspicuous begins to lose its
sense of wildness. In remote places, the stamp of man, unexpectedly
come upon, used to be evidence of the beast in him; makeshift
latrines, ashes of a cooking fire, gnawed animal bones and vegetable
peelings, impressions in the grass where he'd lain. Now, though, the
evidence of his greyer, duller, bureaucratic side is beginning to bellow
everywhere and infect everything; these spindly windmills are a lion-
tamer's whip, implements with which to subdue and harness. We're
losing not just a view but what is truly best in us, and that may very
well turn out to be a tragedy from which we'll never recover. Too, and
specifically here, the wind farms detract from the attractiveness of
Aberystwyth itself; part of the frantic little town's allure was once the
propinquity of it to a wilderness – the offices of diurnal life and their
overbearing punctilio could, within minutes, be escaped from utterly
(albeit temporarily). Now, however, the mountains that surround and
overlook the town are soiled with exactly the matter that they were
once such a refuge from.

In his *Travels With the Flea*, Jim quotes a government spokesman from 1951: 'We intend to plant 800,000 acres in Wales. We intend to change the face of Wales. We know there will be opposition but we intend to force this thing through'. What self-serving short-termism, what arrogance and selfishness, what compensatory assertion of overly-empowered will is in that chilling and disgusting declaration. A vile pronouncement from a vile man. What it meant was that, to quote Jim, 'in a viable, if marginal, agricultural land that, properly managed, was a national resource and in human terms... far more than that, a future desert has been created, its onset assured by tax concessions to the most wealthy in our society, its reality concealed for the moment beneath dense coverage of trees... dark-suited, upright and mutually indistinguishable from Tory politicians'. Think of the plaque at Llyn Fyrnwy which talks of 'impounding the waters' of the rivers Fyrnwy, Marchnant, and Afon Conwy; 'impounding'! For God's sake.

In his essay 'Land and Freedom', Jim points out that many of the wind-turbines in Wales were planted, with Blair's lickspittling approval, of course, by subsidiaries of the Enron Corporation, the 'Bush dynasty's favourite speculators'. This terrifies me; that a distant land, and the imaginative lives of that land's inhabitants, can be altered drastically and forever by those with utterly no idea of the reality of that land or people, their shared history, their common goals. Their sense of continuity – so vital to a sense of present rooted-ness and to a living history – is corroded and ignored by those driven only by stupendous greed (and it is, truly, avarice on a staggering, incomprehensible scale; does another zero really matter at the end of a string of several?).

Once, it was believed that, at the crossroads that intersect the black lakes on the top of Pendam, the *Gwrach y Rhibyn* lay in wait for unwary travellers[13]. 'Gwrach' = 'witch' (you met her counterpart earlier, at Borth bog), and 'rhibyn' = 'streak', which may refer to the ribbon of drool that hung from the hag's warty and whiskery chin (although Holland translates this as 'Hag of the Mists'). She was a terrible entity, her head hooded, beneath which was said to be either an empty darkness or a countenance so awful that to see it would drive a person insane. She would weave and bob in her tattered shawl at crossroads, waiting to suck the blood of innocents through her long, pointed, hollow tongue. But she's not there anymore. Darker demons have ousted her.

PUMLUMON

In a small but mountainous country like Wales, in which the uplands aren't particularly remote places but areas on and amongst which people actually live, towns become linked to mountains (picture the town as the morraine of a great green glacier); so Brecon nestles up to Pen y Fan, Dolgellau to Cadair Idris, Caernarfon and Bangor to Yr Wyddfa itself. Aberystwyth, whilst still possessing the characteristics of a port town, has Pumlumon, the foothills of which could be said, at an admitted stretch, to include Penglais Hill (on which the newer university buildings and National Library stand). It's a big mountain, Pumlumon; not in vertical terms particularly[14], but it's a vast landmass. Its name translates as 'Five Peaks'. It is the source of four rivers (Rheidol and Ystwyth, as you already know, but also the Wye and the Hafren – 'Severn' in English). The towns surrounding it are Llanidloes, Rhaeadr, Newtown, and Aberystwyth. These places are not adjacent to each other.

'Cai and Bedwyr were sitting on top of Pumlumon... in the strongest wind in the world', says *The Mabinogion,* in Sioned Davies's superb new translation. Intervening centuries have done nothing to dampen the ferocity of those winds; it's a wild, shaken, wet and blasted place, up here. George Borrow caught it on a rare sunny day:

> A mountainous wilderness extended on every side, a waste of russet-coloured hills, with here and there a black, craggy summit. No signs of life or cultivation were to be discovered, and the eye might search in vain for a grove or even a single tree. The scene would have been cheerless in the extreme had not a bright sun lighted up the landscape.

Jim Perrin, too, climbed to the summit at a time when 'the high summer sun had sucked the marshes dry, baked quaking bogs into immobility, [and] desiccated even the floating foliage of bogbean'[15]. I've never experienced it like this; I've only ever been flayed by rain up here. Jim goes on: 'The recurrent theme of these hills of mid-Wales is spaciousness, and Pumlumon expresses it to perfection', although he admits to being puzzled, as I am, at Borrow's description of the emptiness of the place; in the mid 1800s the mountain was much more populated than it is now, including at Hyddgen, which Borrow certainly visited (as will you, in a bit). Life does go on up here, on these slopes, in this shrieking wind or pounding rain or throbbing sun. Erwyd Howells, who worked as a shepherd for much of his life up here, collected many stories from friends and family about farming this poor soil and self-published them in his *Good Men and True: The Lives and Tales of the Shepherds of Mid-Wales*. It's well worth a look; there's the Patagonian sheep-lassoer, the snows that fell so thick that telephone wires were at knee-height, Alf the Postman who survived Mametz Wood in World War One. There's the brutality of life up here in the corvids that feed on the lambs even as they're being born, but also the surprising longevity of the people who smoked a lot of rough tobacco and drank a lot of raw ale and spirit yet who adjudged a death in the early seventies as a tragically early one (unless, of course, they'd already committed suicide at the loss of their livelihood in blizzard or flood or lightning bolt). A fresh but frugal diet and active lifestyle works wonders for the heart.

The Edgar Morgan-edited collection *Bro'r Mawn a'r Mwyn*[16] has a more elegiac mood, decrying the fact that the area's particular and meaningful names – of cottage, hill, stream etc. – are vanishing and need to be recorded. It's largely a photographic record, this book, with images not just of a gone wildness but also a gone civilisation; the mines are no more, nor are the shops and chapels and hostelries that catered for their workforce. One photograph of a tombstone in Ysbyty Cynfyn churchyard tells a terrible tale; on 17th February 1856 four babies were born to Margaret Hughes at Nantsyddin, and by the end of that month all had died, and on March 1st her five year old son followed them. On the 6th March her thirty-two year old husband Isaac committed suicide through grief and then, four days later, Margaret's daughter Hannah died, too. Causes of death are not given; it's as if a malicious weather decided to settle on Nantsyddin that month. Ken Jones, in his beautiful book of haiku and haibun[17] *Stallion's Crag* (which, incidentally, thanks Erwyd Howells as an 'authority on the folk history of north Ceredigion'), writes this epitaph for the tragic Hughes's:

> Bone hard chill
> long dead griefs
> chiselled in the stones

Not far away, in Ystumtuen, Sir John Rhys was born, at Aberceiro Fach in 1840. Completely self-taught, he became the leading Celtic scholar of his day, eventually becoming Principal of Jesus College,

Oxford. An extraordinary achievement. So the mountain visits abrupt heartbreak or gradual triumph on those born on its flanks.

You'll find Hyddgen on the Pumlumon massif, too, site of one of Glyndŵr's famous victories. It draws writers and poets and artists to it even though it's commemorated by a singularly unassuming plaque and the huge hydro-electric dam there has changed the landscape of the valley beyond all recognition, despite the fact that very little is known of the battle's details except that 120 of Owain's men defeated a force of 1, 500 English regulars and Flemish mercenaries. David Moore, in his The Welsh Wars of Independence, simply says of it that 'still in Powys, [Owain] defeated the King's troops at Mynydd Hyddgen, and the Welsh flocked to his cause when he subsequently moved into Cardiganshire', while Nia Williams in her Bloody Britain writes that 'the two [armies] met on the bleak uplands of Pumlumon. Armed with bows, billhooks, axes, pikes, spears and swords, the heavily outnumbered Welshmen employed their favourite tactics of ambush and false retreat, and inflicted a terrible death toll, sealing Glyndŵr's heroic reputation among the Welsh'. Geoffrey Hodges has the most exhaustive account in his Owain Glyndŵr and the War of Independence in the Welsh Borders, referring to the only two surviving accounts of the battle, one by Gruffydd Hiraethog and the other by an anonymous annalist discovered by Thomas Ellis. From what can be pieced together, it appears that the fight took place at the end of May 1401. Owain had made a base in the Pumlumon fastness, from where he sent raiding parties out into central and south Wales. This was ideal defensive ground for guerilla fighters. John Charlton, a commander in Henry IV's army, led 1, 500 men 'of the lowlands of Ceredigion and of Rhos and Penfro... to the mountain with the intent to seize Owen', says Hiraethog, who then appears to imply that Owain attacked them from behind[18]. The Ellis source – a MS known as Peniarth 135 – wrote that Charlton's men 'hemmed [Owain] in on all sides at a place called Mynyddhyddgent, so that he could not possibly get off without fighting at a great disadvantage', and the escape came from the rage and courage of simple desperation, not superior tactics. The two quartz boulders that can be seen on Hyddgen, further up from the plaque, are called Cerrig Cyfarnod Owain Glyn Dŵr, or Owen's Covenant Stones, placed there by persons unknown at a time unknown as a deliberate commemoration.

They're the facts, such as we have them. Poets, of course, are fuelled by other things, and Ken Jones writes of walking through the valley at twilight and noticing two figures ahead of him, one which:

radiated a regal presence even at that distance [and] the other looked
to be in clerical garb. . . . Strolling, conferring, gesturing, they disappeared behind a crag. Some local shepherds refer to "the Prince" as
if he were still a local resident. Perhaps he is[19].

The ever-reliable and ever-quotable Jim Perrin writes:

What the covenant commemorated in those death-symbolising stones
entailed is obvious: The terrible ferocity of warriors with nothing left
to lose but life; the grim determination of their cause's last stand;
recognition, slaughter, and the raven's profit[20].

For my part, I'm pleased to notice the red back of a sleeping fox in
the long grass on the slope, not far from where I'm sitting (interestingly, David Moore has a photograph in his book The Welsh Wars of
Independence of a fox more or less in this very spot). The noise of a
vehicle on the far side of the dam wakes him up and he raises his head
to sleepily look and assess threat. He yawns and I get a swift glimpse
of green eyes and then he falls back asleep again. Little more sensu-
ous than a vulpine stretch and slumber (feline, maybe). That red
promise of rapine. I wonder if he feels the bones boil in the soil at his
paws when he prowls these slopes and hollows. I'm sure he does, but
in a way that I could never even begin to understand.

Climb to the top of the slope behind Owain's boulders and join the
road and follow it west, towards Aberystwyth which, if the weather is
right, you might be able to glimpse glittering at the valley's far end.
On the other side of this slope you'll find Nant y Moch reservoir.
Sheep, freshly shorn and looking somewhat shocked and affronted at
the state of new nudity they've had forced on them, bound bleating
away. Magnificent longhorn cattle crop the grass here; like shaggy
russet tanks, these are, completely unfazed by person or car, the
closest you'll ever come to gazing into the face of an auroch. Nant y
Moch is a huge reservoir, created through the damming of three
rivers; the Hengwm, the Llechwedd-mawr and the Rheidol. It's
another drowned valley, of course, and lives were uprooted and
displaced by these waters, but not on the same criminal scale as
Tryweryn; Erwyd Howells has an account of his two friends leaving
the valley, and being filmed doing so, on 9th October 1961. John
Barnie sees it as a symbol of

a new age for crucifixions. . .
the weight of water at her back

> is the pressure she must resist, arms outstretched. . .
> face stretched above her throat to the sky
> like a Victory for a modern empire recently collapsed
> but living on here[21].

From here, you descend, down into Tal-y-bont. You've been here before. You're leaving the high ground behind. 'Once the town is behind you and you get nearer the sky there is an urge somehow to make something of this', writes Peter Finch in his foreword to *Stallion's Crag*, so you go into the pub to do just that.

Last word on Pumlumon to Ken Jones:

> Sunlight on yellow grasses
> on the map
> empty space for miles

EGLWYS FACH AND YNYS HIR

Don't turn west from Pumlumon's foot, head east, just for a bit. Just go a wee bit beyond Tal-y-bont, to the village of Eglwys Fach, the 'Little Church', where the old Welsh kingdoms of Gwynedd, Deheubarth and Powys all meet. R.S. Thomas lived and worked here, once, between 1954 (when he left Manafan), to 1967 (when he moved to Aberdaron), between the ages of forty-one and fifty-three. Justin Wintle's excellent biography *Furious Interiors* offers much information on this period of the poet's life, how it at first satisfied his search for a 'Welsh church' in which he could preach in that language and provide close proximity to the sea to assuage his yearning for the coastal environment of his upbringing on Ynys Môn. This, in the 1950s and 60s, was real 'Welsh' Wales, declares Wintle, deep Cymru, probably much more than it is now (although it does still retain a strong flavour of that), yet it still sported a few types of what Thomas saw as the worst kind of Englishman – ex-army officers and the like. Thomas himself, however, writes in his autobiography *Neb*[22] about how disappointing he found Eglwys Fach; here, the Welsh language was weak, all of the several large houses were 'in the hands of the English', and there had been much 'intermarrying' between the locals and the incomers 'from places such as Herefordshire'. Thomas Love Peacock, the London-based historical novelist, stayed in the village in 1819 and fell in love with and married a local woman, Jane Gryffyth, coincidentally daughter of the then vicar. The place and episode inspired Peacock to write his *The Misfortunes of Elphin* in 1829, an 'extravaganza' (as Wintle calls it) based on the Taliesin legend (who was supposedly born nearby, in the village of Taliesin). R.S. Thomas found refuge from the Sais-tainted village in the abundant birdlife of the Dyfi estuary and Wintle closes his commentary on Eglwys Fach by hinting at how the place became, for Thomas, 'a village of the damned', which, in my opinion, is a tad hyperbolic; I mean, the military types there who would treat vicars as 'subordinate' treat scruffy Cymro-scouse novelists in that way too, and I quite like Eglwys Fach. Still, Thomas produced four volumes of poetry here,[23] and 'consolidated the literary niche his... verse had carved out for him' (Wintle), and became friends with one of the local principle landowners, Hubert Mappin, who owned the Ynys Hir estate, which is now a huge bird sanctuary on the salt-marshes sloping down to the Dyfi estuary and, if you're in the area, is absolutely worth a visit. It's now owned by the RSPB and encompasses over a thousand acres, containing five rich and distinct habitats (forest, marsh, riparine etc.), and a hide built on a motte-and-bailey castle (the Domen Las hide) dating from 1156. It teems, too; there are redstarts and pied flycatchers and warblers in the hanging oak woodland, cormorants and herons and bitterns on the saltmarsh, mersangers and otters and kingfishers on the streams, and a tumult of wild flowers. All of these can be seen from the network of hides along the trails, the walks between which are mostly flat so you can keep a clear view of the wildlife without your bins steaming up or sweat running into your eyes as you labour uphill. The Ynys Hir Hall and Hotel is deservedly award-winning, too.

The nature reserve itself possesses that liminality so typical of this area. Not only does land gradually become water here but the boundaries are blurred, the thresholds smudged; on the marsh, solidity beneath your feet becomes fluid with no visual or tactile announcement. Debbie Moon, author of the novel *Falling*, scripted a film with similar themaic preoccupations called *True Love (Once Removed)*, directed by Kevin Thomas. Filming actually took place in Iceland, but the visual echoes with this part of mid-Wales are frequent and loud. I spoke to Debbie about liminality, not only elemental, but demographical too; she sees Aberystwyth and its surrounding area as the boundary between north and south Wales, and consequently as a kind of island, an isolated community ('it's the end of the road', she says, a view I heard expressed many times in research for this book).

The film is a time-travelling love story set around a fish-gutting plant on an unnamed coast volcanically black with annealed rock, an eerie and haunting landscape. It's a cracker and, to quote Debbie, it's about 'someone who's constantly poised between choices, between different futures that he may or may not be able to influence, to choose for himself. He's not just on the edges of places or cultures, but entire lives'[24]. So does this area work on the imagination, and time and time over I hear similar views expressed: Unreal Aberystwyth. Constantly flitting, fluctuating between the oneiric and the corporeal. You never entirely know where you are, here, the sea soldifying, the liquefaction of the land. Not entirely. Not really.

A couple of miles towards Aberystwyth from Eglwys Fach, is Ffwrnais (Furnace), a hamlet now, once a larger settlement which grew as an industrial centre around silver refining and the smelting of iron. The furnace is still there, and you can see it from the road, a big barn-like building with a large water-wheel attached, the Einion river waterfall that once powered it crashing whitely and angrily into the dark plunge-pool below. Behind it, and reachable via a narrow lane, lies Cwm Einion, or Artists Valley, named so because of its popularity with nineteenth century landscape painters. Footpaths here will take you back up to Pumlumon, if you wish. Robert Plant, of Led Zeppelin fame, owns property here, as well as sheep, which he used to initial with paint; I've often seen them cropping the fields hereabouts or roaming through the conifers with a big red 'RP' on their sides. So, so often this area seems like something from a dream.

BWLCH NANT YR ARIAN/GOGINAN

It's the 26th March and I'm discombobulated. It happens twice every year, when BST tells us to wind our clocks an hour forwards or back. It knocks me off kilter. It's confusing. It causes accidents. I could get really quite riled about it if there weren't bigger things to get worked up over.

But it means I've missed the kite-feeding at Bwlch Nant yr Arian, the wild birds being fed, because I'm an hour late, because the clocks went back, and only a few stragglers wheel and mewl in the damp sky and through the dripping trees. I've been here before, however, on many occasions, sometimes when the entire visible sky is scribbled over with the flight paths of scores of these majestic birds. At 2 p.m. in the winter and 3 p.m. in the summer, you stand on the near side of

the lake (or in the hide on the far side, if you're early or lucky enough
to get a space) and gawp in awe as huge birds emerge from the thick
conifers or over the sawtoothed ridges to swoop and snatch at the
chunks of meat put out for them on the lake shores. The spectacle is
truly breathtaking; the aerobatics of the hawks, and the high-speed
dogfights of incredible speed and agility, make the scalp and skin
prickle and the pulse race. They're so close. Hundreds of them.
Circling and squealing over the spread red fleshbits until as if at a
pre-arranged signal they swoop, almost as one, grab without landing
and rise skywards lifting food to bill on the wing. It's an astonishing
thing to see.

The Forest Visitor Centre here, operated by Forest Enterprise, has
a system of cameras hidden in the kites' nests, as well as a giant
wooden sculpture of a kite spreadeagled on the outside wall (it also
does a decent bowl of cawl). It's eco-friendly, of course, and
surrounded by wooded hills and ridges latticed with trails for
mountain bikers or walkers. There's a children's play area. Main
attractions, however and of course, are the birds, not only the kites
but the buzzards and merlins and peregrines and owls and harriers
and goshawks as well as the myriad species of passerine, some of
which will eat crumbled bits of Welshcake from your hand on the
plank balcony outside the centre[25]. They've become a symbol of
Wales, now, the red kites, *y barcud goch*, and the highlight of conser-
vational success. Until 1994, the location of breeding birds had been
zealously protected for over a century, but in that year the Kite
Country project was set up, estimating that enough time had elapsed
for us to get over our obsession with seeing the birds as vermin and
obeying the governmental edicts of the sixteenth century which
compulsorised their killing. When they were eradicated from the
cities, they were persecuted as threats to agriculture until, by the late
1800s, there were no breeding pairs left in England or Scotland, and
it was only in mid-Wales, especially in the Tywi or Cothi Valleys,
where they clung on[26]. At that point, some local landowners, with an
eye either on posterity or profit (I doubt both), set up an unofficial
protection programme and slow recovery began and is continuing,
spreading even into southern England in recent years. The kite is
largely a scavenger (but not exclusively; I have witnessed them taking
live prey), and lacks the aggression of the buzzard, say, or even the
raven, and it must wait for those birds to open up a sheep carcass
before it can feed, but the quintessence of wildness is in their effort-
less soaring, their hunched and alert roosting, in their sheer size, and

in the ways in which sunbeams bounce like molten copper off their backs or spread wings. They have a power to stun; their utter grace, the purity of their habits (seen as savagery to some attenuated hearts, hence the need to annihilate them), the sense in which they are completely themselves. The 'kiteness' of the kite would've surely survived the physical destruction of the last one; that they could be made extinct, I can grasp and deplore, logically, but the notion that the world could ever be bereft of 'kiteness' contains a contradiction which I have great difficulty comprehending. I understand the objections of some to the turning into spectacle of these incredible birds, as if they have no autonomy, no use, outside of human utility; but these birds are wild, here, and will seek out other prey. This free food and this agog audience will not tame them. Last year, they didn't turn up in more than single figures for a month, because a flock of sheep had been struck by lightning on a Pendam ridge and the kites would rather have feasted on their barbecued flesh than entertain the craning faces. And anyway – they're alive, aren't they? That counts for something, doesn't it? You can see them and hear them and feel the air being beaten by their wings here at Nant yr Arian.

But I've missed them, today, because of stupid daylight stupid saving stupid time, so I follow the path down the valley into Goginan. Nant yr Arian, by the way, translates into English as 'the stream of silver', and refers to the silver-lead mine at Llywernog, a couple of miles back towards Ponterwyd. This area of northern Ceredigion was, by the late 1800s, a British Klondyke, attracting speculators and investors in the tens of thousands. The mine at Llywernog has been turned into a museum now, containing a mock-up of a working mine,

a large collection of rusted machinery and the deep and dark and dank pit itself, the centrepiece of a half-hour underground tour, not for the claustrophobic. When the weather's right, the stream that runs along the valley floor here can catch the sun and burn silver.

Into Goginan, whose pub, The Druid, is like the pub you'd always envisioned as a kid when you'd be old enough to go into pubs; dark and snug and friendly, a sanctuary, a haven, scrape the world off your boots onto the 'Croeso' mat at the door and leave it there[27]. I was once stranded for several hours in this pub as a blizzard blasted and obliterated the world outside; no better place on the planet to be snowed in. Goginan village itself is unofficially divided into Upper and Lower portions, and a walk down into the valley from the pub and then up again on the far side – so lush this landscape, so deeply green – will take you to the old quarries, the slagheaps and earthworks of the mine, worked for silver from 1620 and then lead in 1840, powered by a steam engine and various water wheels of twelve feet, thirty six feet and forty feet in diameter, with twelve working wheels by 1847, producing 25,000 tons of lead ore and half a million ounces of silver by 1863, with a workforce of over 400 and a shaft 852 feet deep, and now, in 2007, disused, empty, decaying, and creepy as hell. It really is eerie, this place; stories abound, mostly involving the screaming and crying of children heard in the woods, and hackles-raised dogs that snarl and flee as if in sheer terror from, to human eyes, nothing. Also, a beast has been seen here; a large, black creature, panther-like, both skulking at twilight through the trees and chasing sheep across the slopes at glare of noon. In a clearing here some years ago I found a bizarre sculpture; a door, propped upright, covered in scrawled peculiar glyphs, with an empty plastic jerrycan strung by rope on each side. A kind of portal, it looked like, provenance and purpose unknown and never seen again. Don't walk alone in these woods at night-time.

Still, and maybe inevitably, the area breeds creativity. The poet Douglas Houston lived here for a time, in the village of Cwmbrwyno, and the obsolete mining gear roundabout is scattered throughout his work, as it is through the landscape:

> Though the machines are gone,
> The derelict wheelpits, grey spoil-heaps,
> And several crumbled buildings linked by the purposive stream
> Announce lead-mine to one informed...
> But to my list of sites least likely to be further robbed
> This nook some way below Plynlimon
> Is added to become one of the irrefutable Prophets[28]

He lives elsewhere now, but Doug remembers how, from this area, 'on a clear day, from our yard you could see right down the falling spread of intersecting valleys to where [Aberystwyth] shone in sunlight mirrored on the miles of sea beyond it'[29]. He remembers, too, the extensive research he'd carry out in the National Library 'as a freelance hack on reference books', and how 'ascending [the Library's] steps to enter under the Athenian heights of its portico could inspire me with something resembling scholarly purpose even on the bleakest of winter mornings, [and] on leaving at six o'clock chucking out time, the whole of Cardigan Bay could be spread out below, reflecting the fire of a magnificent sunset, surprising and liberating eyes that had been locked on print all day'. He also fondly recalls the Verbals series of poetry events run by Clive Meachen (another Goginan resident), which saw luminaries like Robert Creeley, Peter Porter, Ed Dorn, Sean O'Brien, and Edwin Morgan read at the university. Not all memories, of course, are happy ones; Doug tells me about how 'Aberystwyth has... an inimitable line in weirdos of every stripe and people best avoided', and, having lived here for over a decade, I have to agree, but 'the freezing emptiness of midnight on Bath Street or at one a.m. on Terrace Road confers a deeper intimacy with the social fabric of the place.... It's a beautiful place, and more so than ever to the returning revenant'.

Where would we be without poets? Doug left the area some time ago but it continues to tug at his memory and imagination and his latest collection, *The Welsh Book of the Dead*, is drenched with reference to and regard for this rain- and wind-driven corner of old Europe. Many poems in the collection are 'centrally informed by solitude in settings of town, sea, promenade, etc.', too many, really, to quote, but do yourself a favour and snap up whatever of Doug's work you can find. Then find yourself a quiet table in a corner of a pub and read.

Then there's Caryl Lewis, who won the Welsh Book of the Year award in 2005 with *Martha, Jac a Sianco*, and who lives in Goginan, and who, with Nigel Wells (yet another Goginan ex-pat), co-wrote *Walesland/Gwaliadir* in 2006, a 'poetic exploration of Welsh history'[30] in two languages (Caryl's responsible for the Cymraeg). Nigel had the initial idea, whilst on a two-year sailing trip (he's a seafaring man, and is now harbour-master at Aberaeron), of reacting poetically to John Davies's mammoth work *Hanes Cymru/A History of Wales*[31]. It's an inspired idea executed with great power, although I won't pretend to speak for the Cymraeg, Caryl having more and better Welsh than I ever will. But look at this:

Love lives dubious conceit: land is love
And not till the soul's replete
is one nation-heart complete.
Comfort blanket, winding sheet.

Serch sy'n falchder, serch yw'r tir.
Nes i'r enaid lenwi'n wir
ni all cenedl-galon fyw.
Carthen gysur, amdo yw.

And look at this:

The world's
just dirt and spittle:
You're where you are
or where you know.
Dig a little.

Mae'r byd
yn boer a baw:
rwyt ti lle'r wyt ti
ti yw dy gynefin.
Cloddia.

That echoes in my head as I climb up, back towards the A44. A sign in the window of The Druid tells me that Billy Cobham's playing at the Arts Centre tonight. Who's Billy Cobham? Cloddia.

CAPEL BANGOR AND CWM RHEIDOL: BUTTERFLY FARM

Last stop. You're nearly back where you started from, at the mouth of the twisting river. And it's raining. This is more like autumn than spring, with daffodils struggling to bloom on the roadside verges, and despite the new lambs tottering through the half-light.

Enter Capel Bangor. The Maes Bangor pub is on your left and is always worth a stop, as is the Tynllidiart Arms at the other end of the village with the smallest commercial brewery in the world outside it in a blue sentry box. The beer it produces is, often, perfect. A small group of smokers are sheltering from the rain under an awning at the front of the pub; the Welsh have been called 'Mediterraneans in the rain', to quote Pamela Petro quoting Nancy Banks-Smith quoting René Cutforth[32], and that's apposite, here, with the pavement-table stabs at cafe-

culture while the rain hisses incessantly down. Yet Nonconformism, the polar opposite of Mediterranean sun-scorched loucheness, achieved rapid growth in this village, when Lewis Edwards was born in 1808 at Pwllcenawon. His bust can be seen in the forecourt of Penllwyn Chapel as you enter the village from the west. He was a founder of Bala College, one of Wales's earliest colleges, funded by working people, and his brother Thomas also became a significant figure in Calvinistic Methodism. John Roberts, too, the writer, was also born here, in Tanrhiwfelen. He wrote the first congregational hymn-book and founded the Gymanfa Ganu (Festival of Song).

Nonconformism grew out of Puritanism, an extreme form of Protestantism, in Llanfaches in Monmouthshire, where William Wroth (apt name) and Walter Cradock set up the first dissenting church in 1639. It was suppressed by the insistence on the Act of Uniformity of the re-installed Charles II, until James II passed the Toleration Act in 1689 which meant that the Baptists, Independents and Quakers who made up the bulk of Nonconformist organisations no longer had to meet in secret. Its root aims were noble ones, seeking better education for the common people rather than simply luring them from Anglicanism, but its marriage with Calvinist Methodism, which expressed the 'sovereignty of God in predestination [and] also in closely supervised church and civic life'[33], opened it out to hypocrisy and abuse; if a man was predestined for heaven – and of course a man of the cloth would be – then he could act in whichever way he wished on this earth whilst the laity constantly had to deny themselves in the hope that they too were saved whilst being told time and time over that they were damned to eternal torment. It was this dogma that provoked the wrath of Caradoc Evans, and which can still be seen colouring the darker corners of the Welsh psyche. It's also, in its monochromatic insistence on the simple dualism of human affairs, a pretty dull subject to talk about, so we'll escape to the Magic of Life butterfly house, a few miles down the valley in Cwm Rheidol. Here, in a little tropically heated hut close by the reservoir, butterflies the size of birds will flap around your head and lick honey from your fingers. There are Blue and White Morphos, Orange Barred Sulphurs, White Tree Nymphs, Painted Jezebels, Giant Atlas Moths. There are also African flower mantids, small and white and thorny[34], as still as stone but capable of striking within 1/100th of a second, scalpels mounted on thunderbolts. The Blue Morpho butterflies are so big that they don't flutter – rather, they flex their wings from the shoulders like rays or powerful birds. It's wonderful, here. I'd stay longer if it weren't for the unbearable heat. My camera fogs up and sweat runs into my eyes.

Outside, the sun's made an appearance. I sit in a beam of it and eat sandwiches and watch steam rise from Coed Rheidol, sessile oak woodland, birch and rowan and hazel, bilberry, common cow wheat, ash, wych elm and small-leaved lime. Say those names like spells. Neolithic stone axes have been discovered here, 4,000 years old. Beneath Penllwyn Chapel a Bronze Age burial site was found in 1925, containing cremation ash in a ceramic urn. Roman roads scar the hillsides, visible from the air. The Methodists built the tiny red-brick chapel of Llwynygroes and now the symbols of hydro-electric power dominate the valley and have done since the turn of the last century when corn mill waterwheels were converted to drive generators. Construction of the reservoir here was begun in 1955 and in 1961 the Cwmrheidol hydro-electric power station was producing electricity. There is a 'fish ladder' in the reservoir so that sewin and salmon and trout can make their way downstream to the sea. It rises six metres and has fourteen pools. There is a fish farm here too, alongside the power station, in which trout both brown and rainbow are reared.

But the river seethes with invisible pollutants. Mineral extraction today is strictly monitored, but it wasn't, at one long time; the Castell Lode in this area, at Ystumtuen, contained ores of lead, zinc and copper, but also large depositions of the iron sulphide called mercasite, occurring in some areas as solid metre-thick ribs. Nearly 4,000 tons of it were extracted and sold for the manufacture of sulphuric acid. The major problem with it is its instability in the presence of air and water (which both occur at the sites of cataracts, of course, in large quantities), the reaction with which generates sulphuric acid and iron hydroxide, so the mine drainage in this area is now highly acidified, causing the more stable sulphides such as those of lead and zinc to dissolve also, causing further contamination. So the waters of the Afon Rheidol contain high levels of zinc, lead, copper, cadmium and other heavy metals, all mining-derived. Which means that it's

polluted to buggery, and the fish here often have blackened bodies, curvatures of the spine and various fin-deformations. Environment Agency Wales are looking into it, they say, but the problem is long-term, so any solution will be, too. Senseless. Senseless. Never a lesson learned.

But all I see today is the sun suddenly beating and the green of the trees and the blue of the sky and the water-haze in the air above the rapids. I follow the river inland to the ochre moonscape of the Rheidol mine-workings. Carved into a rock in mid-stream is the legend 'Antiok + Ania'; our Polish friends have even reached this valley, it seems. Also on the rock is a cooked prawn. This seems to mean something, but I don't know what. I could be a world away from Aberystwyth in this place, but the twig I flick into the rushing river will, one day, emerge out into the sea at the harbour, beneath Trefechan Bridge and Pen Dinas' ancient fortifications, between Rummer's wine bar and the old lime kiln.

THE GOOD BRIG CREDO/THE ALBION

The *Albion*, out of Aberystwyth, berthed at Cardigan, New Brunswick, in Canada, on June 11th, 1819. It was followed by the *Good Brig Credo* on 4th April 1848, mastered by John Humphreys, bound for Quebec. They never returned. Mouth of the very twisting river.

Notes

1. As an aside, I once watched a peregrine falcon at its prey in a field. Crows surrounded it, hassling, stabbing, cackling. The falcon would lash out with its claws and hiss but the crows kept at it until it took off. I watched it gain height, circling, as the corvids descended on whatever unfortunate animal had become food, and then in a blink the peregrine swooped low over them, banked and swooped again at tremendous speed, instantly altering the dynamics, turning the crows themselves from victorious and aggressive scavengers into cowering potential prey. They took off, complaining, and the raptor again settled down to

eat. Awesome birds, peregrines.

2. The information sheet I pick up says: 'A petition for licence to hold divine services in non-consecrated buildings was granted to Penrhyncoch in 1863'.
3. See Farmer, 'Works Consulted'.
4. Which itself only reaches 2,468 feet at it's highest. But it seems far bigger. See section following.
5. See Richards, Meleri, 'Works Consulted'.
6. And fringed by trees which, as John Barnie writes in his poem 'I Had Climbed the Long Slope', 'try out leaves above branches and trunks/That will never be more than crippled in the poor soil of these fields'. See *The Confirmation*, 'Works Consulted'.
7. See Dylan Davies (D), 'Works Consulted'.
8. In the same poem referred to in note 7, above. It's a powerful poem. Read it.
9. Very different from, but equally evocative as, Harri Webb's name for the mid-Wales uplands, 'the green desert'.
10. He can be furiously exciting, too, when he wants to be; check out the piece 'Street Illegal' in his *The Climbing Essays*, an account of traversing Cheddar Gorge, alone, having just ingested industrial-sized quantities of cocaine and amphetamine. I don't recommend doing it, but by God it's thrilling to read about.
11. See 'Pumlumon Fawr' in 'Works Consulted'.
12. See his *The End of Nature*, 'Works Consulted'.
13. See Curran, 'Works Consulted'.
14. But old maps show it as a vast looming presence in the middle of Wales, inarguably the loftiest peak (it's actually the thirty-nineth highest in the country); this is due to Welsh maps being drawn to please English sensibilities, and Pumlumon's associations with Owain Glyndŵr greatly inflated it in the Saesneg psyche. Keep reading.
15. From *Travels With the Flea*.
16. A clever title translatable as Land of Peat and Minerals but with further meanings of 'the dear land' and 'the kind land' and an untranslatable pun on 'Land, for peat's (Pete's) sake'. A lot going on there, ey?
17. Japanese poetic forms of strict rules concerning syllabics and metre and imagistic control. Too complicated to explain here.
18. Which, if he did, so what? He was massively outnumbered. This was, in today's parlance, 'assymetrical warfare', which is another phrase for 'mismatch'. Or 'unfair advantage'. Or 'bullying'. Or, even, 'massacre'.
19. From *Stallion's Crag*.
20. From *Travels With the Flea*.
21. From 'Nant-y-Moch' in *At the Salt Hotel*.
22. 'No-one' in English.
23. He also left his mark on the interior of the church, which he and his wife decorated. The pews were painted black. A cast-iron crown of thorns was cast. It all became ascetic, pared, and of a kind of stripped-down simplicity that impresses and moves. Much like Thomas's poetry.
24. From a personal email.
25. Although you should be aware of possible distress; once, trying to tempt a chaffinch with a bit of cheese roll, I was shaken to see the blue blur of a sparrowhawk take the smaller bird from mere yards away. A couple of coins of blood on the wood of the bench and a few seesawing feathers all that was left of the cheeping little creature I'd been coaxing towards me for ten minutes or more. As the cafe supplies you with a quick and easy lunch, so it does the raptor.
26. Scientific research at Nottingham University estimated that, in 1977, the entire population of Welsh kites emanated from one single pregnant female. Birds from Scandinavia were

brought in to enrich the gene pool.

27. Now, like most pubs after the smoking ban came into force, The Druid sports a half-sheltered area outside into which smokers can retreat. These new structures have been remarkable testaments to human ingenuity, but have given rise to more complainers, who find it 'unpleasant' to sit in a beer garden surrounded by smokers, or to walk through a group of them huddled in a pub doorway. As if 'unpleasantness' can ever be banished from human interaction; body odour can be unpleasant, halitosis, certain expressed views, certain tattoos, tombstone teeth. 'Unpleasantness' has always been a large component of having to deal with the human race; it's not fatal. This urge to disinfect and scour and impose will and cleanse the world until it sits lifeless and colourless and safe behind a white picket fence.... It will never happen, of course. The muck of it will always bleed through, and thank God for that. But the motives behind such needs are deeply worrying.

28. From 'W.H. Auden in Cwmbrwyno', in *Hunters in the Snow*.

29. All quotes here from a personal email.

30. As the blurb says.

31. First published by Penguin in 1990 and reprinted and updated many times since then.

32. See Petro, 'Works Consulted'.

33. See Hinnells, 'Works Consulted'.

34. The name of which comes from the Greek 'mantis' meaning 'prophet' because of their praying posture.

THE PHOTOGRAPHS

WORKS CONSULTED

Ackroyd, Peter: *Blake*, Minerva, 1997

Allen, Liz: *Walking the Cardigan Bay Coast*, Kittiwake Press, 2000

Atkinson, Tiffany: *Kink and Particle*, Seren, 2006

Barkham, Patrick: 'Hot Rocks and the Book of Snuff: British Library reveals it's missing list', *Guardian*, 28/03/06

Barnie, John: *At the Salt Hotel*, Gomer, 2003

Barnie, John: *The Confirmation*, Gomer, 1992

Booth, Richard: *My Kingdom of Books*, Y Lolfa, 1999

Borrow, George: *Wild Wales*, Everyman, 1939

Carson, Michael: *Stripping Penguins Bare*, Penguin, Black Swan, 1994

Clews, Roy: *To Dream of Freedom*, Y Lolfa, 2001

Cobb, Richard: *People and Places*, Oxford, 1986

Collins, Richard: *The Land as Viewed from the Sea*, Seren, 2004

Constantine, Mary-Anne: 'In a Very Deranged State: Notes on the Iolo Morgannwg Project', unpublished MS, 2007

Curran, Bob: *Vampires: A Field Guide to Creatures that Stalk the Night*, New Page Books, 2005

Davies, Damien Walford, and Turley, Richard Margraff: *Whiteout*, Parthian, 2006

Davies, Dylan (A): 'Out of Africa in Aber!', *Cambrian News*, 19.1.2006

Davies, Dylan (B): 'Big Cat Alert', *Cambrian News*, 23.11.2006

Davies, Dylan (C): 'Ceredigion group named Drug Team of the Year', *Cambrian News*, 1.6.2006

Davies, Dylan (D): 'Remains of Bronze Age Fort Found', *Cambrian News*, 21.7.2005

Davies, Sioned, trans.: *The Mabinogion*, Oxford, 2007

Davies, Terry: *Borth: A Seaborn Village*, Gwasg Carreg Gwalch, 2004

Duncker, Patricia: *Seven Tales of Sex and Death*, Picador, 2003

Duncker, Patricia: 'Teithio yn Nos Nachtreise' in *A Bit on the Side*, Parthian, 2007

Evans, Caradoc: *The Earth Gives All and Takes All*, Camelot Press, 1946

Evans, Caradoc: *Fury Never Leaves Us*, Poetry Wales Press, 1985

Evans, Caradoc: *Morgan Bible and Journal 1939-44*, Planet, 2006

Fanthorpe, Lionel, and Pawelko, Richard: *Talking Stones*, Gomer, 2003

Farmer, David Hugh: *The Oxford Dictionary of Saints*, Oxford, 1978

Ferris, Paul: *Dylan Thomas: A Biography*, The Dial Press, 1977

Fleischer, Jurgen: *A Short History of Greenland*, Aschehaug Dansk Forlog, 2003

Fowler, Carwyn and Jones, Rhys: 'Crud Cenedlaetholdeb Gymraeg/A Cradle of Welsh Civilisation', unpublished MS, 2006

Francis, Matthew: *Whereabouts*, Rufus Books, 2005

Freeman, Michael: *Aberystwyth: A History and Celebration*, Ottakar's Publishing, 2005

Freeman, Michael: *The Coliseum: The History of a Cinema and Theatre in Pictures*, Cyngor Dosbarth Ceredigion, 1994

Freeman, Michael: *Amgueddfa/Ceredigion/Museum*, Cyngor Dosbarth Ceredigion, no date

Gerald of Wales/Giraldus Cambrensis: *The Journey Through Wales*, Penguin, 1978

Gilbey, John: 'Country Diary: Aberystwyth', *Guardian*, 7.10.2006

Gough, Lucy: *By a Thread and The Raft*, Methuen, 2006

Green, John: *Afon Ystwyth: The Story of a River*, Artery Publications, 2006

Gruffudd, Robat: 'Y Lolfa' in *Our Century*, published by Tal-y-bont Old People's Association, 2002, various authors, distributed free to all residents of Tal-y-bont

Gwilym, Dafydd ap: *Selected Poems*, trans. Rachel Bromwich, Penguin, 1985

Henry, Paul: *The Breath of Sleeping Boys*, Gwasg Carreg Gwalch, 2004

Henry, Paul: *Captive Audience*, Seren, 1996

Henry, Paul: *The Milk Thief*, Seren, 1998

Henry, Paul: *The Slipped Leash*, Seren, 2002

Hinnells, John R. (ed.): *A Dictionary of Religions*, Penguin, 1984

Hodges, Geoffrey: *Owain Glyn D?r and the War of Independence in the Welsh Borders*, Logaston Press, 1995

Hodgson, William Hope: *House on the Borderlands and Other Novels*, Gollancz, 2002

Holland, Richard: *Wales of the Unexpected*, Gwasg Carreg Gwalch, 2005

Houston, Douglas: *Hunters in the Snow*, Bloodaxe, 1994

Houston, Douglas: *The Welsh Book of the Dead*, Seren, 2000

Howells, Erwyd: *Good Men and True*, self-published, 2005

Howells, William Dean: *Seven English Cities,* Kessinger Publishing, no date

Jenkins, J. Geraint: *Ceredigion: Interpreting an Ancient County*, Gwasg Carreg Gwalch, 2005

Joel, Janet: *Nanteos*, Dyfed Cultural Services Department, 2002

Jones, Cynan: *The Long Dry*, Parthian, 2006

Jones, George (ed).: *Mercator Media Forum*, Vol. 6, University of Wales Press, 2006

Jones, Ken, *Stallion's Crag*, Iron Press, 2003

King James Bible with Apocrypha, Oxford, 1997

Lewis, Caryl and Wells, Nigel: *Walesland/Gwaliadir*, Gomer, 2006

Lewis, Gwyneth: *Chaotic Angels*, Bloodaxe, 2005

Lewis, Saunders: *Presenting Saunders Lewis*, ed. Alun Jones and Gwyn Thomas, UCW Press, 1983

Lewis, W.J.: *A Fashionable Watering Place*, Cambrian News Press, no date

Lewis, W.J.: *Born on a Perilous Rock*, Cambrian News Press, 1980

Llanbadarn Fawr Through the Centuries, Cyhoeddwyd gan Cyngor Cymuned

Llanbadarn Fawr, no authorship, 1994

Lycett, Andrew: *Dylan Thomas: A New Life*, Phoenix, 2003

Maycock, Bob, et. al.: *Cambrian Snooze*, various editions, privately printed, 2006/7

McKibben, Bill: *The End of Nature*, Penguin, 1990

Moffat, Alastair: *The Sea Kingdoms*, Harper Collins, 2002

Moon, Debbie: *Falling*, Honno, 2003

Moore, David: *The Welsh Wars of Independence*, Tempus, 2005

Morgan, Edgar, et. al. (eds.): *Bro'r Mawn a'r Mwyn*, Pentre Pumlumon, 2002

Morgan, Eluned: 'Minority Languages in the European Union', Labour European Office, no date

Morgan, Mihangel: *Melog*, trans. Christopher Meredith, Seren, 2005

On Paper, 'An Exhibition of Work by Three Artists', Ceredigion Museum publications, Aberystwyth, 2003

Osmond, John (ed.): *Myths, Memories and Futures: The National Library and National Museum in the Story of Wales*, Institute of Welsh Affairs, 2007

Parker, Mike and Whitfield, Paul: *Rough Guide to Wales*, Rough Guides, 2003

Parker, Mike: *Neighbours From Hell*, Y Lolfa, 2007

'Pencarreg Three: Speeches from Carmarthen Crown Court', Cymdeithas yr Iaith Gymraeg, 1980

Perrin, Jim: *Travels with the Flea*, The Inpinn Press, 2003

Perrin, Jim: *The Climbing Essays*, The Inpinn Press, 2006

Perrin, Jim: 'Pumlumon Fawr', *Guardian* country diary, 10.3.2007

Perrin, Jim: 'Land and Freedom' in *New Welsh Review*, winter 2006

Petro, Pamela: *Travels in an Old Tongue*, Flamingo, 1997

'Poet from Middle Ages gets the backing of politicians', uncredited article, *Cambrian News*, 2.11.2006

Poster, Jem: *Courting Shadows*, Sceptre, 2002

Poster, Jem: *Rifling Paradise*, Sceptre, 2006

Pryce, Malcolm: quoted in article 'Sea-front may soon be a distant memory', *Cambrian News*, 27.10. 2005

Pryce, Malcolm: *Aberystwyth Mon Amour*, Bloomsbury, 2001

Pryce, Malcolm: *Last Tango in Aberystwyth*, Bloomsbury, 2003

Pryce, Malcolm: *The Unbearable Lightness of Being in Aberystwyth*, Bloomsbury, 2005

Richards, Meleri: *Spirit of the Miners* newsletter, Countryside Council for Wales, 2006

Robinson, David and Platt, Colin: *Strata Florida Abbey/Talley Abbey*, Cadw, 1998

Rodway, Simon: 'Flag Waving', unpublished MS

Rogers, Byron: *The Bank Manager and the Holy Grail*, Aurum Press, 2005

Sampson, Fiona: *The Distance Between Us*, Seren, 2005

Sampson, Fiona: *Folding the Real*, Seren, 2001

Smith-Twiddy, Helen: *Celtic Cookbook*, Y Lolfa, 1985

St. Padarn's Church, Penglais School History Society, Waunfawr, Aberystwyth, no accredited author, no date

Tanner, Marcus: *The Last of the Celts*, Yale UP, 2004

Thomas, Ben Bowen: *'Aber': 1872-1972*, University of Wales Press, 1972

Thomas, Ned: *The Welsh Extremist*, Y Lolfa, 1991

Thomas, R.S.: *Autobiographies*, trans. Davies, J.W., Phoenix, 1997

Thomas, R.S.: *Selected Prose*, Poetry Wales Press, 1986

Transcript promotional material, Mercator Centre, Aberystwyth, 2000 and onwards

Troughton, William: *Aberystwyth Voices*, Tempus, 2000

Williams, Gwyn A.: *When Was Wales?*, Pelican, 1985

Williams, Herbert: *Ghost Country*, Gomer, 1991

Williams, Herbert: *The Woman in Back Row*, Gomer, 2000

Williams, Hywel: 'The Great Redeemer', *Guardian*, 7.12.2005

Williams, Nia, et. al.: *Bloody Britain: A History of Murder, Mayhem and Massacre*, AA Publishing, 2002

Wintle, Justin: *Furious Interiors*, Flamingo, 1997

Yardley, Evan: *Five O'Clock Shadows*, The Book Guild, 1988

Y Lolfa publisher's catalogue, 2005

Y Lolfa, *Y Byd: Papur Dyddiol Cenedlaethol* promotional material, 2005 (?)

WEBSITES

www.aber.co.uk

www.aberystywth-online.com

www.babylonwales.veryweird.com

www.book-of-thoth.com

www.cambriansnooze@lists.riseup.net

www.canysrufus@siopsgidie.fsnet.co.uk

www.geocities.com/janjoeluk/Nanteos_Mansion

www.haxan.com

www.idler.co.uk/crap

www.lit.across-frontiers.org

www.llgc.org.uk

www.nanteos.co.uk

www.news.bbc.c.uk/wales

www.spirit-of-the-miners.org.uk

www.statistics.gov.uk

www.stpadarns@llanbadarn.org.uk

www.thecarvery.net

www.themodernantiquarian.com

INDEX

ACKNOWLEDGEMENTS

Our thanks to the poets for permission to include their work.

'Black Lion Prophet' by Tiffany Atkinson is taken from *Kink and Particle* (Seren, 2006).

'A4' by Damian Walford Davies is taken from *Whiteout,* co-authored with Richard Marggraf Turley (Parthian Books, 2006).

Both 'Starlings' and 'Bronze Angel' appear in Matthew Francis's collection *Whereabouts* (Rufus Books, 2005).

'Marine Terrace', from which an excerpt is taken, appears in Paul Henry's colelction *The Slipped Leash* (Seren, 2002).

As the text states, the passage of poetry by Matthew Jarvis is excerpted from 'An Aberystwyth Canto'.

Gwyneth Lewis's poems 'Buoys' and 'Cenetneary Greetings from the National Library of Wales' are as yet uncollected. The latter was specially commissioned by the National Library of Wales as part of its extensive centenary celebrations.

The two excerpts by Nigel Wells and Caryl Lewis are taken from *Walesland/Gwaliadir* (Gomer, 2006).

'Hill Fort' by Herbert Williams cis to be found in his collection *Wrestling in Mud* (Cinnamon Press, 2007).

THE AUTHOR

Niall Griffiths was born in Liverpool in 1966, studied English, and now lives and works in Aberystwyth.

His novels include: *Grits* (2000), *Sheepshagger* (2001, *Kelly & Victor* (2002); *Stump* (2003), and *Runt* (2006). *Stump* won the Welsh Book of the Year. *Grits* was made into a film for television, and *Kelly & Victor* and *Stump* are also being made into films.

Niall Griffiths has also written travel pieces, restaurant and book reviews, and radio plays. His next book will be a further volume in the Real series, on Liverpool (2008).